The Euro-dollar Market and the International Financial System

Geoffrey Bell is a Director of Schroder International Ltd., the London merchant bank. In addition, he is a special columnist for *The Times* and writes regularly on international and domestic financial problems.

He was born in 1939 and was educated in Grimsby and at the London School of Economics. He joined H.M. Treasury after graduation as an Assistant Economic Adviser and in 1963/4 spent nine months as a Visiting Economist with the Federal Reserve System, mainly at the Federal Reserve Bank of St. Louis. Between 1964 and 1966 he lectured on monetary economics at the London School of Economics and acted as an Assistant Adviser at H.M. Treasury. In 1966 he became Economic Adviser to the British Embassy in Washington, where he stayed until joining Schroder's in 1969.

He has published numerous articles on domestic and international finance in academic journals as well as his regular features in *The Times*. He has also contributed to three books on monetary economics.

The Euro-dollar Market and the International Financial System

Geoffrey Bell

A HALSTED PRESS BOOK

JOHN WILEY & SONS
NEW YORK - TORONTO

© Presses Universitaires de France 1973

All rights reserved. No part of this publication may be reproduced or transmitted, in any form or by any means, without permission.

First published as *Les Marchés d'eurodevises*
by Presses Universitaires de France 1973

Published in the United Kingdom 1973 by
THE MACMILLAN PRESS LTD
Published in the U.S.A. and Canada by
Halsted Press, a Division of
John Wiley & Sons Inc., New York

First edition 1973
Reprinted 1974

Library of Congress Cataloging in Publication Data
Bell, Geoffrey, 1939—
    The euro-dollar market and the international finance system.

"First published as Les Marchés d'eurodevises ... 1973."
"A Halsted Press book."
Bibliography: p.
    1. Euro-dollar market.   2. International finance.
I. Title.
HG3881.B44313   332.4'5   73-12683
ISBN 0-470-06405-6

Printed in Great Britain

To the Memory of my Father

Contents

	Preface	ix
1	Introduction	1
2	Origins and Institutional Mechanics	7
3	Growth, Size and Structure of the Market	18
4	Changing, Lending and Borrowing Techniques	32
5	Credit Creation and the Euro-dollar Market	42
6	U.S. Monetary Policy: U.S. Banks and the Euro-dollar Market	54
7	National Monetary and Exchange Rate Policies	67
8	The Breakdown of the Bretton Woods International Financial System and the Impact of the Euro-dollar Market	83
9	The Next Phase	96
	Appendix A	111
	Appendix B	117
	Appendix C	118
	Further Reading	119
	Index	123

Preface

The purpose of this short book is to examine the growth of the euro-dollar market and its relationship to the functioning of the international financial system as a whole. The aim has been to blend economic analysis with the practical problems of international monetary relations and the field of international banking and finance. My excuse for writing this book was the dramatic change in the system heralded by President Nixon's announcement of the suspension of the convertibility of the dollar into gold on 15 August 1971 and followed by two devaluations of the dollar, one in December 1971 and the second in February 1973. Watersheds in history are, to put it mildly, a useful starting point for any re-examination of the past and reassessment of the future.

In writing this book, I have drawn on my experiences in Government, in academia, and, more recently, as a practising banker. My thanks are due to my colleagues in each of these fields, from whom I have drawn heavily both as sources for new ideas and as sounding boards for my own views. In particular, I am grateful to Herbert Christie, who has been most helpful in reading the draft and giving suggestions. *The Times Business News* has been extremely generous in allowing me space to write on international financial problems and my thanks are due to Hugh Stephenson and Peter Jay.

Finally, my sincerest thanks go to my secretary, Mrs Audrey Simmons, who has given her talents most ably and her time most willingly in the preparation of this work.

April 1973   GEOFFREY BELL

1 Introduction

The international financial system underwent a more or less continuous series of crises from 1964, culminating on 15 August 1971 with President Nixon's decision to suspend the convertibility of dollars into gold. The Smithsonian Agreement of December 1971 involved a first devaluation of the dollar and this was followed in February 1973 by a second devaluation of the dollar, amidst a flood of currency speculation. After the foreign exchange markets reopened following the 1973 devaluation of the dollar, most advanced industrial countries moved over formally to a system of floating exchange rates. Six of the nine E.E.C. countries – Germany, France, the Netherlands, Belgium, Luxembourg and Denmark – adopted a collective joint float against the dollar while the pound, the Italian lira, the Swiss franc and the Austrian schilling floated independently; as did the Japanese yen and the Canadian dollar. In other words, any semblance of the International Monetary Fund world of fixed exchange rates disappeared after a temporary re-emergence in 1972 following the Smithsonian Agreement. This represents an enormous change in the international financial system, especially in relation to the stated policies of most governments and central banks which have been wedded to a system of fixed exchange rates but who found the pressure of currency movements too much to handle by any means other than by adopting floating exchange rates. And this system, with countries tending to go their own way in exchange rate policies except for limited co-operation within the E.E.C., looks like being the pattern that will hold for the foreseeable future.

The collapse of the Bretton Woods world was largely determined by the inability of the system to deal with the problem of the balance of payments imbalance of the United States *vis-à-vis* the rest of the world. At the same time, the underlying malaise of the system was brought into both sharp relief and up to breaking point by the weight of short-term capital movements emanating from the euro-currency markets. In 1971 the 'underlying' balance of payments deficit of the United States amounted to around $10 billion, but the actual increase in dollar holdings of foreign official institutions was close to $30 billion with the effect of capital movements magnifying the underlying problem threefold. Similarly, in the latter part of January and the early part of February 1973, approximately $9 billion was taken in by central banks, with the German Bundesbank having to buy over $6 billion in a vain attempt to maintain a fixed parity for the Deutschemark. These flows of funds against the dollar would have been even greater had it not been for the strength of exchange rate restrictions surrounding Japan and other countries in Western Europe.

Over the years the international money markets have facilitated movements of funds out of weak currencies and into strong currencies, but the scale and the immediacy of these movements has grown immeasurably alongside the expansion of the euro-currency markets. In fact the tremendous increase in the market within the last two years has been determined in no small part by speculative demands for dollars, which could be sold with consumate ease for other currencies. The die was cast after 1967, but it took another four years or so before governments realised that their defences against currency movements were totally insufficient to maintain a system of fixed parities and, once asset holders realised that they could force governments to exchange rates against their will, the day of floating exchange rates had arrived.

At the present time the euro-currency market is probably in excess of $110 billion and has provided the mechanism by which the world's money markets during the 1960s became inter-related to a degree not seen before in the international financial system. For example, branches of U.S. banks were able to borrow $15 billion of short-term funds from the market in 1969, and this had effect of exporting tight money conditions and the high interest rates prevailing in the United States to the rest of the world. Moreover, the repayment of these borrowings in 1970 and 1971 resulted directly in inflows of dollars into Western Europe which, in turn, helped to generate expectations in the market that decisive action would have to be taken to stem this flood of dollars and that any action would necessarily include widespread currency revaluations. Yet once exchange rates had been generally adjusted upwards against the dollar in December 1971, then, instead of dampening subsequent speculation against the dollar, this pressure was abated only temporarily; as witnessed by the events of 1973, especially when the United States balance of trade account failed to improve as rapidly as expected.

The problem facing the central banks of Western Europe and Japan was that the inflows of dollars within a world of fixed exchange rates resulted in sharp expansions in their domestic money supplies, which the authorities were anxious to avoid. The initial reaction of central banks was to introduce widespread exchange control devices designed to prevent local banks from taking non-resident deposits, and local European and Japanese companies from being able to borrow in the euro-currency markets and switch these funds into domestic currencies. These measures were obviously only partly successful, given that it is extremely difficult to prevent waves of capital movements from taking place in anticipation of imminent exchange rate adjustments simply through exchange control techniques. This is because banks and companies borrowing dollars and buying other currencies are quite willing to pay very high interest rates on dollar borrowings and receive even negative interest rates on their non-dollar assets if the spot rate for dollars is expected to decline. The only way of stemming these movements effectively is to allow the buying pressure of non-dollar currencies to be reflected in an upward movement in those exchange rates, with the central banks standing back from the foreign exchange market. As a consequence, central banks then refrain from adding to their domestic money supplies by selling local currencies in an attempt to maintain a pre-determined exchange rate against the dollar. Put another way, the need has been to insulate the domestic money markets from the international markets and this cannot be achieved in a world of fixed interest rates and relatively free capital movements.

Given the sharp deterioration in the United States balance-of-payments position on the current and long-term capital account beginning in the second half of the 1960s, there is no doubt that an impasse would have been reached sooner or later involving a major realignment of currencies. However, it can be argued with some strength that the timing of President Nixon's decision to suspend the convertibility of the dollar was prompted by the impact of currency flows against the dollar. More recently, the 1973 crisis had its origins in a combination of two factors – concern that the United States balance of payments was simply not improving fast enough; and by the impact of currency fears feeding on themselves.

On 22 January the Italian Government decided to introduce a two-tier exchange rate system which led to heavy outflows of funds from Italy into Switzerland, and the Swiss authorities decided to allow their exchange rates to float rather than buy these additional funds. Despite the fact that the initial run against the dollar was at some stages removed from concern about the dollar *per se*, this triggered off a general reaction in the foreign exchange markets culminating in a widespread floating of exchange rates.

Whatever the antecedents of these series of crises, governments are now clearly determined to restrict the ability of asset holders to move funds freely across exchange boundaries in order to try and prevent a recurrence of these problems. Governments have redoubled their efforts to restrict international money flows through a combination of exchange controls, and by allowing currencies to find their own level in the markets. Above all it has become crystal clear that the international financial system in general, and the balance-of-payments adjustment process in particular, cannot be expected to function smoothly if the euro-currency market were to be allowed to remain in an unfettered state. This has widespread implications for the future of the market and for the banks participating in the market.

Future of the market

All the indications point to a period of slower growth for the euro-dollar market in the next few years, especially regarding transactions within Western Europe and the United States. In the past banks operating in the euro-currency market have been able to service local companies in most of the domestic money markets of Europe by supplying dollars, usually from London, which could be freely converted into Deutschemarks, Swiss francs and the like. Now exchange control regulations prevent these movements of funds so that it is difficult, if not totally impossible, to arbitrage funds between the international money market and local money markets. As a result, if banks are to service adequately multi-national companies with subsidiaries in all or most

European countries, banks must have access to local sources of finance in the future – they can no longer operate from their 'off-shore' banking centres. This means that banks will require a presence in each of the separate money markets of Europe, and to achieve this end they will be forced to merge or amalgamate with other banks, or set up their own operations.

Similarly, a large source of demand for euro-dollar borrowing has resulted from the restrictions on the U.S. balance of payment on capital account, which has meant that U.S. companies have been forced to borrow funds abroad for investment purposes rather than transfer dollars directly from the United States. In addition U.S. banks themselves have been extremely limited in the amount of dollars that they could transfer abroad because of Federal Reserve guideline restrictions, which was the reason why they set up branches in Nassau and London to gain access to external dollars. Yet at the same time as the Secretary to the Treasury, George Schultz, announced the 10 per cent devaluation of the dollar in February 1973, he stated that a decision had been taken to phase out these controls on capital movements. This termination of U.S. capital controls will mean that U.S. companies will turn increasingly to domestic sources of finance for their external requirements, and U.S. banks will be in a better position to furnish these companies' financing needs from within the United States. Hence, the combination of restrictions on the free movement of monies in Western Europe and the relaxation of U.S. capital controls will remove a major source of demand for euro-currency borrowings.

A corollary of this argument is that in the future the geographical thrust of the euro-currency market will change. Already euro-currency loans to areas outside of Western Europe have been growing rapidly and this can be expected to continue. Lending to Latin America, Africa and the Middle East from London-based banks increased by over $6 billion in the twelve months to October 1972. This raises a particularly important point about the future structure of the market. As borrowers from the less developed nations of the world become more important, an increasing proportion of the funds channelled from the market are likely to be used for investment in long-term capital projects and so bankers will necessarily have become more expert in the financing of these projects. Rather than having a market which has been primarily dominated by Western European and U.S. multinational companies with unquestionable names, the question of credit assessment is becoming both more difficult and more important. Loans to countries outside Western Europe are typically medium or longer term, so that the maturity structure of loans is tending to lengthen apace while, on the other hand, the maturity structure of deposits has not grown *pari passu*, and this might lead to liquidity problems as time goes by. In addition, bankers who are successful in operating in these newer areas of business are likely to find it advantageous to establish operations physically closer to the geographical bases of the borrowing companies, and hence the euro-currency market looks like becoming more regionally biased. Already Singapore has become an important centre of euro-currency activities with the bias of their loans being in the Far East, and the chances are that other such centres will grow in importance so long as the utilisation of funds in Western Europe remains limited. Consequently, just as banks wanting to service clients within Western Europe will have to establish operations in each of the countries of that area, so they will need to have subsidiaries or associated companies in the newly emergent regional centres of the euro-currency market.

This does not necessarily mean that there will be an absolute reduction in London's euro-currency activities, but it does mean that there will be a change in direction in lending business and that the pre-eminence of London as a centre for euro-currency business will become less pronounced with the growth of more regional centres. The market itself looks like entering a period of less rapid growth unless there is another series of currency crises involving the dollar, giving rise to renewed speculative demands for borrowing – but this now looks less likely against a background of the recent upward movement of currencies against the dollar and the introduction of floating exchange rates.

2 Origins and Institutional Mechanics

The international money and capital markets are markets for lending and borrowing dollars and other currencies outside their countries of origin. By far the most important of the international money markets is located in Europe and is referred to as the 'euro-currency' market. As the majority of transactions takes place in dollars the market is usually described as the 'euro-dollar' market, even though most major currencies are traded. It should be emphasised that the term 'euro' is by no means exclusive, as trading in U.S. dollars and other currencies takes place in Canada, the Lebanon, Nassau, Panama and the Far East. Nevertheless, as the bulk of dollars traded outside the boundaries of the United States occurs in Europe (and mainly in London), the shorthand description 'euro-dollar market' is a pretty accurate description for the world's international money market, except that the centres outside of Europe have grown in importance during the last two years. Over the last dozen years or so this market has become the primary means of transmitting short-term funds across national boundaries and, more recently, medium- and longer-term funds.

At the long end of the liquidity spectrum the market for ten- to fifteen-year loans is called the 'euro-bond' market and is separate, although related, to the euro-dollar market. This market for international capital is of a more recent vintage and has really only been a significant factor in the raising of funds since 1968. Just as in the shorter-term market, funds flow into and out of the euro-bond market from all corners of the globe, but the institutions making up the market are mainly based in Europe. Again, various currencies are traded, with bonds being denominated in dollars, Deutschemarks, Swiss francs and guilders as well as composite units of account. The relative importance of bonds denominated in one currency or another has varied a good deal depending on general concern about the future value of those currencies but, over time, the market for dollar bonds has been the most important. Despite the recent growth of the euro-bond market, there is no doubt that it remains (and is likely to continue to remain) the weak sister in comparison to the euro-dollar market.

Origins

Some form of international money market has existed for a long period of time and a highly-developed market existed before and after the First World War, with London as the focal centre. After the Second World War a number of European banks (particularly U.K. banks) revived the practice of taking dollar deposits and, instead of placing these dollars in New York, lent them out to other European banks to finance international trade. As a result a market began to develop for dollars outside New York. Every historian of international money markets has his pet reason accounting for the real thrust which launched the euro-dollar market, but the one most usually cited is the action of various state banks in Eastern Europe placing dollars with the Moscow Narodny Bank in London and the Banque Commerciale pour L'Europe du Nord in Paris. These state banks supposedly preferred to keep their dollar balances safe in Europe rather than run the risk of having the balances blocked in New York. As these dollar balances grew, banks made every effort to lend out these funds at more attractive yields than could be obtained by the usual operation of investing the dollars in the New York market.

The sterling crisis of 1957 gave the market a fillip as the use of sterling for financing foreign trade was severely limited. This encouraged British Banks to turn to dollars as a substitute for sterling in order to keep their position in the financing of world trade. More generally the introduction of non-resident convertibility throughout Western Europe at the end of 1958, and the relaxation of exchange controls, paved the way for the development of the euro-dollar market. Banks were then able to switch in and out of currencies (other than their own) so giving them the basis on which to expand their international financing transactions. Even so, whatever the euro-dollar market's antecedents were, the fundamental reason why the market has flourished is because the banks operating in the market (euro-banks)* have been able to establish interest rates at levels which have been extremely com-

* The term 'euro-bank' is simply used as a shorthand description for those banks taking and lending euro-dollars.

petitive against their domestic banking counterparts on both sides of the Atlantic. At the same time, United States and European monetary authorities have been of invaluable assistance (if only by accident) in the development of the market through their introduction of a wide variety of artificial barriers to the free flow of funds across national boundaries.

The ability of banks operating in the euro-dollar market to work on smaller margins between lending and borrowing rates than their domestic competitors has been the result of a number of factors. In the first place the banks have been free of the type of self-imposed regulations common in virtually all domestic money markets. Each country usually suffers from some form of cartel arrangement among banks such as those relating to the levels of interest rates offered on deposit and charged on loans. Similarly domestic banks often limit the type of business which they will undertake, as in the case of self-imposed limits on the maturity terms of loans or deposits. As a result the euro-banks have the opportunity of circumventing these restrictions and so attracting business both in terms of cost and in terms of maturity. A second factor operating to the advantage of euro-banks has been the absence of reserve requirements against deposits traded in the market. Virtually all domestic banking systems have obligatory reserve requirements for deposits in one form or another. Sometimes banks are obliged to hold cash reserves in central banks against deposits which yield zero interest or, at best, hold a proportion of their deposits in the form of government securities which typically offer relatively low yields. As a result the effective cost of taking deposits is increased or, put the other way round, the interest rate that these banks can pay on funds is reduced in comparison with the situation where no reserve requirements are levied. On the other hand euro-dollar deposits are free of these reserve requirements and so banks can offer more attractive rates. In addition some countries, particularly the United States, forbid the payment of interest on deposits with a maturity of less than thirty days. This ruling was the result of the chaotic conditions of the 1930s which led to unsound banking practices in that country. But the inability of U.S. banks to pay interest on deposits with a maturity of less than one month has given euro-banks an open door to attract deposits by paying interest on deposits with maturities of between one and thirty days.

Again, throughout the decade of the 1960s the Federal Reserve Board of the United States set a ceiling on the rate of interest that U.S. banks were able to pay on time deposits with maturities greater than 30 days. This was the so-called Regulation Q of the Federal Reserve which, from time to time, undoubtedly gave a great impetus to the development of the euro-dollar market. Throughout most of the last decade interest rates in Europe were higher than interest rates in the United States, and so those banks were able to attract dollar deposits by offering higher yields than were available on the western shores of the Atlantic. The existence of Regulation Q was not of major significance in this respect for much of the period; the ceilings were not operative because existing money market rates in New York were below the permitted ceilings. However, the fact that Regulation Q was extant did deprive U.S. banks of the chance of offering more attractive rates had they wished to compete with euro-dollar banks.

More importantly, it was in periods of 'tight money' in the United States that the Regulation Q ceiling acted as a major stimulus to the euro-dollar market. In 1966 and in 1969 the Federal Reserve reduced the rate of growth of the money supply, which had the effect of forcing up money market rates in that country. However, at the same time the Q ceiling prevented banks from raising their interest rates on deposits and so deposit rates became extremely unattractive, with the result that banks experienced withdrawals of deposits. In order to try and regain those deposits U.S. banks increased their borrowings of dollars in the euro-dollar market, which forced up interest rates in that market. This raising of euro-dollar rates, in turn, persuaded more and more investors who had held deposits and government securities directly in the United States, to redeposit those funds in the euro-dollar market and take advantage of the attractive yields prevailing.

Nevertheless, although many observers felt that the abolition by the Federal Reserve of the Regulation Q ceiling would destroy the euro-dollar market, these fears were groundless. The Regulation Q ceiling did, on occasion, stimulate the growth of the euro-dollar market, but this was not the fundamental reason for its development; that reason was the market's freedom from controls.

The same basic factors accounting for the growth of the euro-dollar market have also applied on the lending side of the balance sheet. Euro-banks have been able to lend dollars and other currencies at lower rates than domestic banks because of the incidence of interest rate limits established formally or informally within national boundaries. At the same time the demand for borrowing in the euro-dollar market (and euro-bond market) was given a very great fillip through the introduction of direct and indirect exchange controls in the United States. As early as 1963 the introduction of the Interest Equalisation Tax effectively closed the New York capital market for foreign borrowers, who had to turn elsewhere for capital. In February 1965 the U.S. Administration instituted a voluntary programme aimed at protecting the balance of payments by limiting the expansion of foreign assets held by U.S. commercial banks and other financial institutions. Essentially this programme restricted the ability of these institutions to transfer dollars from the United States to companies abroad wishing to borrow. As the U.S. balance of payments deficit continued to deteriorate, these controls were strengthened and on 1 January 1968 mandatory controls were introduced on U.S. direct investment abroad. To all intents and purposes this meant that U.S. companies wishing to invest overseas (and particularly in Western Europe) had to raise the required funds outside the United States – and the obvious place was the euro-dollar market. For longer-term funds U.S. companies turned to the euro-bond market and this was, perhaps, the most important factor in the development of that source of long-term funds. The names of the U.S. corporations seeking funds were sufficiently attractive to persuade European investors to resist investing in the New York capital market directly and take advantage of buying bonds on their own doorstep.

More recently the demand for euro-dollars has been increased by investors wishing to benefit from differing interest rate levels among money-market centres. As interest rate levels have moved out of line, both within the major European countries and between Europe and the United States, it has been profitable on occasion for investors to borrow dollars and switch to other currencies – namely, to indulge in interest arbitrage. This factor became particularly important in 1970 and 1971 when large-scale arbitrage took place between the euro-dollar market and German and U.K. money markets. Related to this demand for funds has been the phenomenon of currency speculation. As it became more obvious over time that the U.S. dollar was over-valued relative to the European currencies, expectations of upward movements, particularly of the Deutschemark, became widespread. Consequently investors found it profitable to borrow dollars from the euro-market and sell these dollars for Deutschemarks and other currencies, and take the profits on subsequent revaluations. This source of demand for euro-dollars has been intermittent but intense as currency crises have repeated themselves.

Finally, the role of the U.S. balance-of-payments deficit itself in the development of the euro-dollar market should be introduced. This is an area which has been misunderstood as there has tended to be a widespread view that if and when the U.S. balance-of-payments deficit were reduced, then in line with this the euro-dollar market must also decline. The essential point is that the outflow of dollars from the United States, associated with the payments deficit, gave people outside the United States the chance of putting those dollars back in New York or investing them elsewhere. In many countries, recipients of dollars (e.g. exporters) had no choice but to surrender those dollars to central banks in return for local currency. However, enough of these dollar-holders have been free to choose the location of their investment outlet, including central banks themselves, and this is where the euro-dollar market has offered an attractive alternative.

Thus, even if the basic balance of payments position of the United States were in balance, dollar-holders around the world may still be attracted by the yields ruling in the euro-dollar market and so be persuaded to place their funds there rather than in New York. In other words the U.S. balance-of-payments deficit has helped to fuel the euro-dollar market but has not been critical in its development.

Institutional mechanics

The euro-dollar market is entirely of a wholesale nature and transactions are typically of a minimum size of $1 million although sometimes smaller, and are confined mainly to the very highest 'names' with low credit risks. The market has its international framework in a network of international banks connected by correspondent relationships and linked by telephone and telex. As the market developed during the 1960s, the number

Origins and Institutional Mechanics 13

of participating banks rose sharply. Most obvious has been the growing numbers of U.S. banks entering the market via the establishment of branches, particularly in London but also elsewhere in Europe. At the same time more and more European banks have found it profitable to borrow and lend euro-dollar funds so the scale of European participation has risen. This has been partly the result of the senior management of banks overcoming their initial suspicion that the market would be simply a passing phase; the fact that the market has flourished helped to allay the fears of even the most conservative bankers. More importantly, the increasing scale of demand for external funds has meant that banks have had to turn to the market to supply their customers or else lose business. In addition throughout most of the last decade British banks were severely limited in their domestic lending activities by the Bank of England's controls over the amount that any one bank could lend to U.K. borrowers. Checked on this front, banks found that they had to focus their attention on dollar business if they were to continue expanding their scale of operations. This factor applied to many banks on the continent of Europe as well.

The focal centre of the market is undoubtedly London where about 50 per cent of euro-currency transactions take place, although the predominance of London has declined slightly in the last couple of years. The pre-eminence of London as the centre of the market largely stems from the long tradition of international banking in the United Kingdom, originating from the days when sterling, and not the dollar, was the world's main trading currency and reserve asset. U.K. banks switched over smoothly and easily from financing international financial transactions in sterling to doing the same in dollars; it is the skill of knowing how to do business and having established customers which matters much more than the particular form of currency that is financing the transactions. Since the second half of the 1960s the role of U.S. branches has contributed a very great deal to the relative importance of London in the market. The attraction of London as a centre for U.S. banks was mainly because of its background as an international money market with available skilled personnel and freedom from controls. But once banks began to establish themselves the process naturally tended to snowball. Nevertheless, non-economic factors such as a common language and the like surely helped in re-establishing London as the world's major international money centre despite the declining role of sterling and all the balance-of-payments problems of the United Kingdom.

Banks operating in the market act as intermediaries between investors (who may be central banks, companies or individuals) depositing funds, and ultimate borrowers. There is no such phenomenon as 'free' deposits in the market because chequing accounts do not exist as in a domestic banking system. All deposits are interest-bearing whether they have a maturity of one day or several years. In terms of numbers of transactions, the vast majority is accounted for by movements of funds among the banks themselves. These inter-bank deposit movements reflect a variety of forces operating in the market. Banks use the market as a means of adjusting their liquidity position, taking deposits when their balance sheet becomes illiquid and putting the deposits out when the liquidity structure of their book becomes excessive. Again, banks buy or sell deposits depending on their view of the future movement of interest rates. In this case they will increase the level of deposits if interest rates are expected to rise at some future date, or reduce deposits when the opposite movement is anticipated. Similarly, banks will increase their dollar positions in order to switch into another currency (e.g. the Deutschemark) if it is felt that the exchange value of other currencies will rise or reverse the process if the exchange value of non-dollar currencies is expected to fall.

Yet, cutting through this myriad of transactions, the main purpose of banks taking deposits is to lend to commercial borrowers. These borrowers may be companies financing exports or imports, or simply borrowing for working capital purposes in any number of countries. The bank makes funds available in dollars or other currencies depending on the cost and/or availability and the borrowing company then uses these funds to sell for local currency finance activities in France, the United Kingdom or elsewhere. Often the end-user of funds might not be a manufacturing company but a local or municipal authority, or a public utility such as the U.K. Electricity Council or Gas Board, and U.S. banks have been major end-borrowers themselves in order to remit funds back to the United States for use by their head offices.

The euro-dollar banking process might best be clarified by the following schematic presentation:

(1) A holder of a $1 million deposit (A) in a U.S. bank is attracted by the interest yield on a deposit in the euro-dollar market. First, the holder allows the time deposit to mature so it becomes a demand deposit in the United States and then the funds are transferred to Europe. So (A)'s demand deposit in the U.S. bank falls, while Euro-bank I's demand deposit increases.

U.S. BANK ($m)

Liabilities	Assets
Demand Deposits	
− 1m. (A)	
+ 1m. Euro-bank I	
Net change 0	0

EURO-BANK I

Liabilities	Assets
Time Deposits	Demand Deposits
+ 1m. (A)	+ 1m. (Demand deposit U.S. bank)
Net change + 1m.	+ 1m.

Demand deposits in the U.S. banking system (and hence the U.S. money supply) remain unchanged but, through the intermediation of the Euro-bank, a dollar denominated deposit has been created in the euro-dollar market. Given that the holder (A) regards this deposit as a perfectly acceptable substitute for the time deposit previously held with the U.S. bank, then the world supply of 'dollars' has been increased by this transfer of funds. However, it should be stressed that the euro-dollar deposit cannot be used for settling debts through the writing of cheques – it is simply a liquid asset.

(2) Euro-bank I will be anxious to convert its demand deposit (non interest bearing) into an interest bearing asset by using the deposit to lend out. Let us assume that the entire $1 million is on-lent to another Euro-bank which is in temporary need of funds and is consequently willing to offer a slightly higher rate than Euro-bank I paid for those funds. (In practice, Euro-bank I would keep some small proportion of the demand deposit in reserve but that does not affect the process.) Euro-bank I instructs

the U.S. bank to debit its demand deposit and credit the account of Euro-bank II. Again, the U.S. banking system is left unaffected.

U.S. BANK ($m.)

Liabilities	Assets
Demand Deposits	
— 1m. Euro-bank I	
+ 1m. Euro-bank II	
Net change 0	0

EURO-BANK I

Liabilities	Assets
	— 1m. (Demand deposit U.S. bank)
	+ 1m. (Time deposit Euro-bank II)
Net change 0	0

EURO-BANK II

Liabilities	Assets
+ 1m. (Time deposit Eurobank I)	+ 1m. (Demand deposit U.S. bank)
Net change + 1m.	+ 1m.

Thus, Euro-bank I, in the same manner as (A), has converted a demand deposit into a time deposit but by so doing has brought into existence another $1 million of dollar denominated deposits, bringing the total of euro-dollar deposits to $2 million. This process may be repeated a number of times with deposits being transferred among banks with the number of 'dollars' growing proportionately. Obversely, when the deposits mature (unless renewed), the chain unwinds itself. These inter-bank transactions clearly inflate the statistical level of deposits in the market as a number of banks may claim essentially the same deposit as its own. As a result, these deposits are netted out for statistical purposes in examining the growth and size of the euro-dollar market.

(3) The next step is when Euro-bank II lends to a commercial customer for (say) working capital purposes in France. As before, Euro-bank II will instruct the U.S. bank to debit its demand

deposit and credit the account of the commercial borrower. In this case, Euro-bank II has converted its assets from a demand deposit with the U.S. bank into a loan (or, in practice, a proportion of the deposit).

EURO-BANK II ($m.)

Liabilities		Assets
		− 1m. (Demand deposit U.S. bank)
		+ 1m. (Commercial loan)
Net change	0	0

U.S. BANK

Liabilities		Assets
Demand Deposits		
− 1m. Euro-bank II		
+ 1m. Commercial borrower		
− 1m. Commercial borrower		
+ 1m. Banque de France		
Net change	0	0

The commercial borrower may use these dollars now lodged in the U.S. banking system to buy francs for use at home in France and so sells the dollars in the foreign exchange market with the result that the demand deposit is reduced yet again and the dollars finish in the hands of the Banque de France (which has sold the francs for the dollars). As the central bank will usually leave the dollars in the United States, either on deposit with the U.S. bank in the form of a time deposit or purchase a U.S. Treasury bill, the euro-dollar chain comes to an end. This is because the process of putting the deposits back into the euro-dollar market through a euro-bank has ceased. However, it is possible that the central bank might choose to convert its new inflow of dollars into a euro-dollar deposit and so the chain of deposit creation continues —but more about that later. The essential point to note is that each euro-dollar transaction is reflected in a movement in U.S. demand deposits even though the actual trading takes place in Europe.

3 Growth, Size and Structure of the Market

The euro-currency market has grown at a truly phenomenal rate; a rate beyond the wildest estimates of even the most farseeing of forecasters. At the end of 1972 the market exceeded $100 billion net of the duplication of deposits with perhaps up to three-quarters of deposits in dollars, and this size has been reached from a level not much exceeding $1 billion in 1957/8. It is difficult to conceive of any similar expansion of a major market, especially with the rate of growth accelerating over time. Partly because of the rapid expansion in operations, there is no statistical series available covering the period from the early beginnings to the present. The principal collector of statistics and 'market watcher' is the Bank for International Settlements in Basle. However, the B.I.S. did not begin to keep a more or less complete track of the dollar and foreign currency transactions of European banks until 1963 and, by that time, the market had achieved a substantial size.

As a result, the only way of going back to the late 1950s is to use statistical series of the external liabilities of banks in the United Kingdom prepared by the Bank of England. Even so, it was not until 1962 that the Bank of England began publishing a series showing the external claims and liabilities of U.K. banks in dollars and covering the activities of all banks in Britain, including the branches of U.S. banks (Table 1 and Chart 1).

Given the relative importance of London in the euro-dollar market, which may be seen by comparing the B.I.S. numbers for all European banks (Table 2) with Table 1, the Bank of England series gives a fairly accurate record of the growth of the market. Using other figures published by the Bank of England, it appears that the market amounted to about $1 billion (excluding the other overseas business of U.K. banks) by the end of 1957, and by 1962 deposits had more than doubled. Thereafter the level of dollar liabilities of U.K. banks virtually doubled over each successive two-year period. Up to 1970 the rate of growth fluctuated year by year but, on balance, accelerated. Between the end of 1963 and

Growth, Size and Structure of the Market

TABLE 1

External Liabilities and Claims of U.K. Banks in U.S. Dollars 1962/72

Period ending December	Liabilities $m	Claims $m
1962	2,475	2,248
1963	3,002	2,870
1964	4,371	3,696
1965	5,261	4,547
1966	7,591	7,311
1967	9,561	9,189
1968	15,370	14,988
1969	25,747	25,234
1970	31,406	29,254
1971	36,139	33,415
1972	48,252	45,642

Source: *Bank of England Quarterly Bulletins.*
N.B. Non-dollar currency liabilities at 31 December 1972 were $11,564 m. and claims $10,803 m., making total liabilities $59,816 m. and claims $56,445 m.

CHART 1

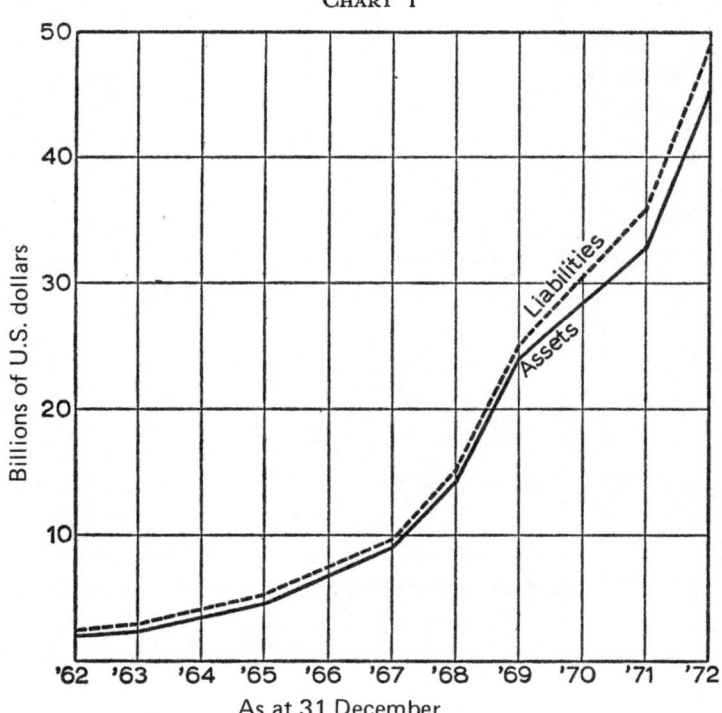

As at 31 December

TABLE 2

External Positions of Reporting European Banks in dollars and certain other Foreign Currencies

In millions of U.S. dollars

	Dollars					Other foreign currencies				
	vis-à-vis			vis-à-vis					of which	
	banks	non-banks	Total	banks	non-banks	Total*	D-mark	Swiss francs	Pounds sterling
End of										
Liabilities										
1964			9,650			2,570				
1965			11,390			2,820				
1966	10,640	4,130	14,770	3,060	510	3,570	970	1,220	710
1967	13,440	4,680	18,120	3,680	470	4,150	1,670	1,400	800
1968	20,630	6,240	26,870	5,620	1,040	6,660	3,010	2,290	800
1969	35,740	10,460	46,200	8,850	1,320	10,170	4,640	4,030	810
1970	47,460	11,240	58,700	13,550	2,320	15,870	8,080	5,720	940
1971	60,770	9,980	70,750	24,130	2,750	26,980	14,630	7,760	2,110
1972	84,920	11,810	96,730	31,580	3,620	35,200	19,540	8,810	2,210
Assets										
1964			9,000			3,030				
1965			11,580			3,550				
1966	13,970	2,100	16,070	3,150	690	3,840	1,420	930	800
1967	16,460	3,430	19,890	3,720	850	4,570	2,060	1,110	870
1968	25,280	5,150	30,430	5,480	1,500	6,980	3,920	1,820	610
1969	41,540	6,090	47,630	8,030	2,160	10,190	5,990	2,980	580
1970	48,520	11,850	60,370	13,210	4,670	17,880	10,110	5,080	610
1971	57,140	14,360	71,500	21,880	6,750	28,630	16,720	8,180	1,620
1972	79,660	18,340	98,000	25,840	8,000	33,840	20,400	7,780	2,180

* Including, in addition to the currencies given separately, French francs, guilders and lire.
Source: Bank for International Settlements, *Annual Reports*.

the end of 1965 U.K. banks' gross foreign currency liabilities to overseas residents increased by over 25 per cent per annum but, in the next three years up to the end of 1968, the average rate of increase climbed to nearly 50 per cent per annum, and during 1969 there was an increase of 75 per cent. The rate of increase fell back in 1970 and 1971 as U.S. banks repaid dollar borrowings as monetary conditions eased in the United States, but once again the growth rate picked up in 1972.

Since 1963 the B.I.S. has been publishing data covering the entire euro-dollar market. Short-term dollar and foreign currency liabilities and assets on non-residents are collected for commercial banks operating in ten countries: Belgium and Luxembourg, France, Germany, Italy, Netherlands, Sweden, Switzerland, United Kingdom, Canada and Japan (Table 2 and Chart 2).

CHART 2

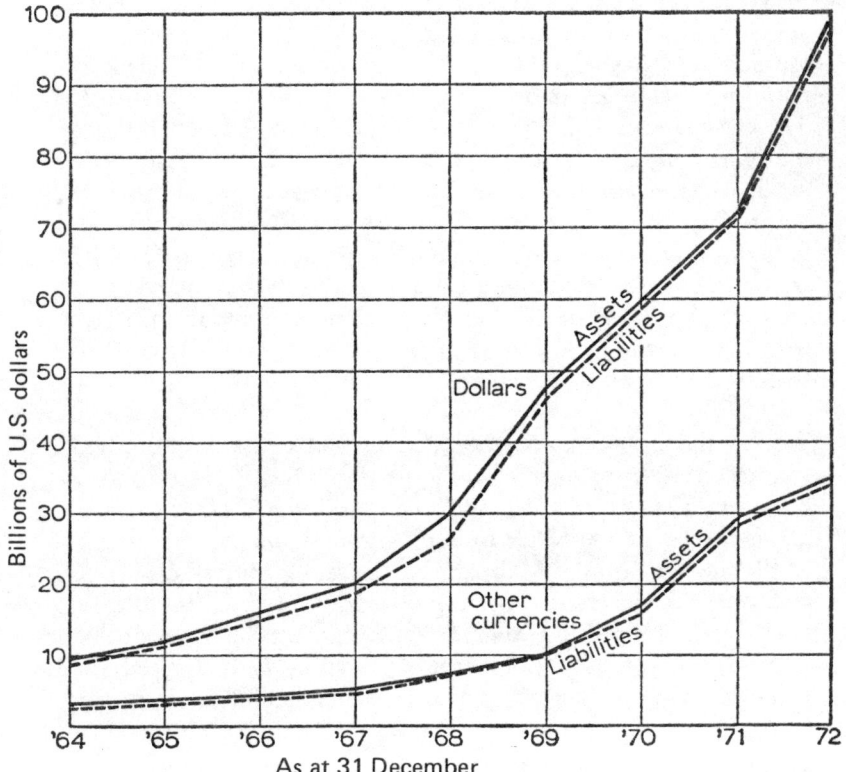

There are various statistical problems with this series despite the considerable efforts of the B.I.S. to eliminate the pitfalls where possible. The main one is that of double-counting deposits, as it is virtually impossible to completely net-out interbank deposit transactions which blow up the size of reported dollar deposits. These numbers therefore overstate the size of the market although not necessarily the rate of expansion over the period.

One of the most interesting features which comes out in Table 2 is that the relative importance of dollar transactions began to diminish in 1969 and this trend accelerated in 1970 and 1971. This partly reflected the repayment of dollars by U.S. banks which particularly affected the activities of U.S. branches in London. Whereas in 1969 these branches had been the big takers of dollars to plough back to their head offices, in 1970 they were forced to look elsewhere for lending opportunities. On the other hand the demands for borrowing in Europe (with dollars being converted for local currencies) accelerated sharply and especially in Germany (in addition United Kingdom borrowings rose markedly until the Bank of England prevented U.K. residents taking euro-dollars for less than five years from January 1971). These European demands for funds mainly resulted from the fact that euro-dollar interest rates fell sharply in 1970 so that borrowing in that market became more attractive on a cost basis than borrowing in domestic European markets. The non-dollar component of the market rose even more rapidly in 1971 as fears grew about the dollar exchange rate and investors scrambled to buy Deutschemarks, Swiss francs and other non-dollar currencies, with even sterling showing a sharp increase, all in expectation of revaluations against the dollar.

Taking the period as a whole (as in Table 2), the euro-dollar market grew from over $8 billion from the end of 1963 to $97 billion by the end of 1972, and to $133 billion if other currencies are included in the total. But this figure overstates the true size of the market because of the double-counting of deposits between banks in the different reporting countries. Netting out these deposits as far as possible and allowing only a proportion of dollar liabilities and assets of European banks *vis-à-vis* the United States to be included in the euro-dollar market, the B.I.S. estimated in its 1972 Annual Report that the total volume of euro-currency credit amounted to $91 billion with dollars accounting for $70 billion of that total (Table 3). On a comparable basis, the B.I.S. estimated the dollar component of the market to be approximately $9 billion by the end of 1964 and this had risen to $14.5 billion by the end of 1966 and $25 billion by the end of 1968. Over the next two years the market increased a little over another $25 billion to $46 billion. More recently the B.I.S. has improved its estimates of the non-dollar component of the market and suggests that at the end of 1972 other currencies traded in the market amounted to $21 billion, of which Deutschemarks were by far the most important.

These estimates do not include the euro-currency business of banks outside of Europe such as in Singapore etc. except to the extent that their activities are channeled through reporting European banks. If the activities of these banks are included then at the end of 1972 the total size of the market is increased by about $15 billion to over $100 billion.

Sources and uses

Depositors of foreign currencies may be divided into four categories: official institutions (including central banks); governments and international organisations; international and domestic companies; commercial banks and individuals (i.e. those not short of money). Central banks maintain dollars as part of their international reserves and some of these banks are not above the temptation of earning a higher rate of return on their balances by putting funds in the euro-dollar market rather than leaving them in New York. This also happens indirectly as European central banks deposit a part of their funds with the B.I.S. and that institution, in turn, has put dollars into the market. Usually this is a harmless enough practice but it certainly did a great deal of damage in 1970 and early 1971. European central banks were experiencing big inflows of dollars because of interest-arbitrage operations but, instead of allowing this pressure to force up euro-dollar interest rates as dollars were syphoned off the euro-dollar market, these central banks calmly put the dollars straight back into the market! This meant, in effect, that the euro-dollar credit-creation process could continue unbroken or, put the other way, the central banks were helping to perpetuate the interest-rate dif-

TABLE 3

Sources and Uses of Euro-dollars

	End of 1964	1965	1966	1967	1968 ($ billions)	1969	Including Other Currencies 1970	1971	1972
Sources									
U.S. and Canada	1.5	1.3	1.7	2.6	4.5	6.7 (*4.1)	(*4.5)	(*6.1)	(*6.9)
Japan	—	—	—	—	0.1	0.4			
Eastern Europe	0.3	0.3	0.4	0.5	0.6	1.0			
Other	2.8	3.3	4.0	4.8	6.6	10.8			
Total	4.6	4.9	6.1	7.9	11.8	18.9	29.3	38.6	56.8
Reporting European area									
Non-banks	1.8	2.2	2.8	3.9	5.2	9.4	14.2	16.0	17.8
Banks	2.6	4.4	5.6	5.7	8.0	9.2	13.5	16.4	16.4
Total	4.4	6.6	8.4	9.6	13.2	18.6	27.7	32.4	34.2
Grand Total	9.0	11.5	14.5	17.5	25.0	37.5	57.0	71.0	91.0
Users									
U.S. and Canada	2.2	2.7	5.0	5.8	10.2	17.8 (*16.5)	(*13.1)	(*8.3)	(*9.6)
Japan	0.4	0.5	0.6	1.0	1.7	1.5			
Eastern Europe	0.5	0.5	0.7	0.8	0.9	1.0			
Other	0.9	1.5	1.9	3.0	4.2	5.5			
Total	4.0	5.2	8.2	10.6	17.0	25.8	33.0	38.2	53.1

Growth, Size and Structure of the Market 25

Reporting European area									
Non-banks	2.3	3.3	3.7	4.1	4.7	5.6	15.0	19.1	20.8
Banks	2.7	3.0	2.6	2.8	3.3	6.1	9.0	13.7	17.1
Total	5.0	6.3	6.3	6.9	8.0	11.7	24.0	32.8	37.9
Grand Total	9.0	11.5	14.5	17.5	25.0	37.5	57.0	71.0	91.0
Net									
U.S. and Canada	†0.7	†1.4	†3.3	†3.2	†5.7	†11.1	†(*8.6)	+2.2	+2.7
Japan	†0.4	†0.5	†0.6	†1.0	†1.6	†(*12.0)			
Eastern Europe	†0.2	†0.2	†0.3	†0.3	†0.3	†1.1			
Other	−1.9	−1.8	−2.1	−1.8	−2.4	−5.3			
Total	−0.6	†0.3	†2.1	†2.7	†5.2	†6.9	†3.7	−0.4	−3.7
Reporting European area									
Non-banks	†0.5	†1.1	†0.9	†0.2	−0.5	−3.8	+0.8	+3.1	+3.0
Banks	†0.1	−1.4	−3.0	−2.9	−4.7	−3.1	−4.5	−2.7	+0.7
Total	†0.6	−0.3	−2.1	−2.7	−5.2	−6.9	−3.7	+0.4	+3.7

* U.S. only.
† Indication that the area of grouping in question is a net user of Euro-dollar funds, whereas a minus sign indicates that it is a net supplier.
Source: Bank for International Settlements, *Annual Reports*.

ferential between the euro-dollar market and domestic markets, so encouraging increasing inflows of dollars into their coffers.

More deliberately, central banks have, on occasion, used the euro-dollar market as a means of regulating domestic money-market conditions. The German central bank has, from time to time, offered German commercial banks attractive swap arrangements in order that banks would borrow dollars from the Bundesbank. Under these arrangements commercial banks buy spot dollars for Deutschemarks and the central bank agrees to buy the dollars back at an attractive rate at a future date. The combination of the interest yield on the dollar asset by investing in the euro-dollar market and the spot-forward exchange deal gives the banks a more attractive return than can be obtained within Germany. [The advantage to the central bank is that the domestic money supply is reduced as commercial banks surrender Deutschemarks to buy dollars, while, at the same time, its dollar holdings are reduced. The process may be reversed when central banks wish to expand rapidly their domestic money supplies, but this is a rare occurrence.]

The advantages of the market to commercial companies which have temporary excess funds are threefold. There is the attraction of higher yields than can be obtained elsewhere and for a wider range of maturities; the attraction that banks will tailor deposits to suit the maturity convenience of the customer so that if the company wants to be back in cash on a particular future date, then this can be easily arranged; and seeing that most international transactions (and hence payment flows) are denominated in dollars, there is the attraction of minimising exchange risks. Of course, companies are always able to switch their excess dollars into other currencies but this exposes them to an exchange risk (as well as a potential advantage on revaluations). In addition, the markets other than that in euro-dollars are extremely limited in the choice and availability of assets except in the United States and United Kingdom. The same factors apply to individuals with excess funds although, in total amount, it is doubtful that individuals account for a very significant proportion of funds flowing into the market. Commercial banks use the market as depositors when they have excess liquidity, although the injection of funds by one bank is cancelled by the taking of funds by another. However, during periods when central banks are offering inducements to invest in the market through swap arrangements, commercial banks are net suppliers of funds to the market.

As may be imagined, it is very difficult to assess the relative importance of the separate types of investors in the market, especially as their respective importance almost certainly varies over time. According to the B.I.S. and Oscar Altman,* in the early years of the market official institutions were the largest suppliers of funds. Over the middle years the importance of international companies tended to grow, but during the last two years or so official institutions have once again become the major net suppliers of funds. Certainly there is little doubt that in 1970 the primary suppliers of funds to the market were central banks taking advantage of higher interest rates.

As may be seen from Table 3, the geographical sources of funds deposited in the euro-dollar market have varied a good deal since 1964. At the end of 1964 countries outside of Western Europe ('Reporting European Area' being composed of the eight major nations in Western Europe itself. However, over the next three years the main net injection of funds came from Europe, largely reflecting the growing balance of payments surpluses of that area. Yet, since the end of 1968, it has been the rest of the world that has become the most important source of funds to the market. Deposits from the United States rose sharply in 1968 as U.S. companies borrowed heavily in the euro-bond market, taking long-term funds and investing the proceeds temporarily in the money market. More importantly, central banks and government institutions in Latin America and the Middle East have become more and more attracted by the relative interest rates available in the market and so have redeposited their dollar reserves in Europe. Similarly some part (and perhaps a substantial part) of the reserves of Sterling Area countries previously held in the United Kingdom before the British devaluation in 1967, were placed in the market over this period.

By and large central banks do not borrow funds from the eurodollar market. However, governments and local authorities have been substantial takers of funds, both short- and long-term. Local authorities in the United Kingdom offer short-term assets which

* 'Recent Developments in Foreign Markets for Dollars and Other Currencies', *International Monetary Fund Staff Papers*, VIII (1963) pp. 48–96.

often attract investors to borrow euro-dollars and switch into sterling for on-lending to these institutions while covering the transaction in the forward market. In addition, public utilities in the United Kingdom and other countries have had recourse to euro-dollar (and other currency) borrowings, taking advantage of the cost differential between that market and the domestic money and capital markets. For such borrowings, the domestic monetary authorities have, from time to time, insured these bodies against the exchange risk of dollar borrowing. More recently, governments and state-controlled entities of the less developed parts of the world have become very large takers of funds from the market. Thus the 'rest of the world' has become the biggest element in the market on both sides of the balance sheet.

Over the longer period, commercial non-bank customers such as international corporations have been the large takers of euro-dollars both on grounds of cost and, since the tightening of the United States' balance-of-payments programme in 1968, on grounds of necessity. Thus banks participating in the market have tended to look to business corporations of United States and European parentage as primary sources of business.

One of the single biggest sources of demand for euro-dollars in the history of the market was that of U.S. banks attempting to evade the Federal Reserve's tight money policies in 1966 and, more importantly, in 1969. At the peak of borrowing in August 1969, U.S. banks were taking nearly $15 billion from the euro-dollar market. This figure had been building up from 1965 but showed its biggest increase in 1969 at the height of the squeeze on credit in the United States. As conditions eased in the second half of 1970, these borrowings were repaid and this accounted for the reduction in the net borrowing position of the United States in that period.

Thus, as shown in Table 3, the United States built itself up as the major taker of euro-dollars until 1970, with Western Europe being the major provider of funds. The pattern of borrowing changed dramatically in 1970 as the United States repaid borrowings and Western Europe began to emerge as a very substantial taker of funds.

One aspect of the demand for euro-dollars by U.S. banks was that it enhanced the relative position for London in the market as most U.S. banks used their London branches as the prime means of buying dollars to retransmit to their respective head offices. Similarly the expansion in the size of operations of U.S. branches in London meant that their position in comparison with the London Clearing Bank and merchant banks grew. According to a survey by the Bank of England* at the end of 1963, three groups of banks together accounted for two-thirds of the currency business undertaken in the London market; these were the American banks, the British overseas and Commonwealth banks (each accounting for about 25 per cent of the total), and the merchant banks (rather less than 20 per cent). However, by the end of 1969 the relative share of U.S. branches had risen to 54 per cent, with the number of branches increasing by twenty.

By the end of 1972 the number of U.S. branches had risen to thirty-eight along with a growing number of consortia banks in which U.S. banks, both with and without branches in London, participated. This desire to open branches in London was not prompted by any significant part, since 1969, by the desire to tap euro-dollar funds and repatriate these back to the head offices (that could be achieved more cheaply from a branch in Nassau). The main reason for the opening of branches by U.S. banks with assets down to not much more than $1 billion, has been prompted by the competitive position within the United States as well as the need to follow their customers abroad. If one bank in an area has a branch in London, the chances are that its main competitors will have to think very hard about following suit or take the chance of losing out at home!

Maturity of liabilities and claims

The Bank of England has begun to analyse the maturity distribution of the liabilities and assets of London-based banks operating in the eurocurrency market. The reports submitted to the Bank of England confirm that the maturity of claims has lengthened in recent years but that this increased maturity on the assets side of the balance sheet has not been matched by an equivalent increase in the maturity of deposits. Even so, 85 per cent of the assets of these banks had maturities of less than one year at October 1972 – but this figure has to be interpreted with care. A large propor-

* 'The euro-currency business of banks in London', *Bank of England Quarterly Bulletin*, vol. 10, no. 1, (Mar 1970) pp. 31–49.

tion of bank claims represent short-term loans made in the London inter-bank money market (usually through the purchase of certificates of deposit issued by other banks) which reduces the entire maturity structure of total assets. Moreover, the proportion of such money market instruments has grown sharply for many banks operating in the market as lending opportunities have become scarcer in 1971 and 1972. On the other hand the maturity structure of commercial loans has definitely lengthened markedly as business has become more difficult and banks have turned increasingly away from the United States and Western Europe to make loans to less developed countries needing funds for project financing. This trend may be expected to continue.

Foreign Currency Liabilities and Claims of U.K.-based Banks — October 1972

	(Percentages)	
	Liabilities	Claims
Sight	11	9
Less than 8 days	7	5
8 days to 3 months	49	44
3 months to 1 year	27	27
1 year to 3 years	3	7
3 years and over	3	8
	100	100

Source: *Bank of England Quarterly Bulletin* (Mar. 1973).

Sources of speculation

Perhaps the most intriguing aspect of the market has been that of identifying the sources of currency speculation largely because most operators in the market deny that they indulge in speculative activities. The multi-national corporations are usually vociferous in their denials of participating in speculation – especially against the dollar when the multi-nationals are United States owned! But despite protestations of innocence, the fact is that enormous flows of funds do take place out of one currency (usually the dollar) and into others, with the Deutschemark being most in demand. However, it is impossible to document the sources of speculation within the private sector as the transactions are put through banks which naturally are unwilling to release the names of the companies and bodies ordering such operations. Also, any one bank would have little idea of the total currency operations of its clients as the larger clients would use several banks. On the other hand, central banks should have a good idea of switches in the currency position of official institutions except if any of these transactions are channelled through commercial banks, which is more than likely.

Moreover, what is 'speculation' to the central bank experiencing sharp inflows or outflows of funds is more often than not regarded as 'hedging' on the part of the body moving the funds. If a multi-national company has assets in a country whose currency is expected to depreciate in value, then that company will wish to protect the value of its total assets by borrowing in that currency and selling the currency for a strong one, either spot or forward. Similarly, if a company has future payments to make in a currency which is likely to appreciate in value, then that company will naturally speed up its payments or try to protect itself by borrowing in a weak currency and buying the strong currency. What is generally regarded as outright speculation is when the entity selling one currency for another is not actually covering a risk but aiming to make a net profit. A bank or company having had dollar deposits but no Deutschemark liabilities may well have been tempted to sell those dollars for Deutschemarks (or add to the profit by borrowing dollars as well) and so finishing up with a greater amount of dollars subsequent to the Deutschemark revaluations. But if governments and central banks delay making exchange rate changes until the movements become not only predictable but have to be of a significant size, then operators on the foreign currency markets would have to be paragons of virtue to sit back and do nothing.

The fact is that all types of bodies using the euro-currency market have indulged in speculation although not, of course, every bank, company or individual. Many banks have found that their foreign exchange departments have been significant sources of profit, just as the treasury departments of multi-national companies. Also, a number of central banks (other than the Group of Ten) have sold part of their dollar holdings for other currencies as a part of their policy of reducing their potential exchange risk even at times of currency crisis, so adding to the degree of pressure on currencies.

4 Changing, Lending and Borrowing Techniques

It would be an exaggeration to argue that the sophistication of banking practices within the euro-dollar market have risen in direct proportion to the absolute growth of the market. Nevertheless, the flexibility in terms of amounts, maturities, forms of debt instruments and the like, in banking practices, has grown immeasurably over the last few years. In the early days loans typically had maturities of only a few months, but now loans are made for periods up to ten years and, occasionally, beyond, especially now that Japanese banks have entered the market in a major way. Also loans are made in a wide variety of currencies. Recently, loans in excess of $100 million have become a common feature of the market, with even larger loans occurring on an increasing scale. For example, British Petroleum alone raised a £360 million ten-year loan (of which about half was in dollars and the rest in sterling) for the development of the Forties Field in the North Sea in June 1972. A particularly interesting feature of this loan was that the security offered to the lenders was the oil reserves and not the credit of British Petroleum itself.

At the same time, the margins between the cost of funds to banks and the rate of interest on loans to high-grade commercial customers have declined sharply with growing competition. (Some bankers argue, to vanishing point.) Another milestone in the development of the euro-dollar market was reached in 1970 when the first placements of euro-dollar commercial paper were announced. Even though the amounts of paper placed were small, this marked a breach in to the total domination of commercial banks over lending and borrowing at the short end of the market.

For a long time the euro-dollar market remained underdeveloped in that the alternatives to borrowing and lending, except through commercial banks, remained limited, unlike within developed money markets, but now borrowers have a wide choice between bank loans, commercial paper and medium-term private note placements. More importantly, there is often a substantial imbalance between the size (in terms of net worth or a similar index) of the commercial or governmental borrowing entities and the banks providing the credits. There is a wide disparity in the size of banks' lending funds but, by and large, most of the banks are of medium or small size although the big banks have the greatest proportion of the business. For example, few banks could lend an individual company $25 million or more from their own resources without running into serious problems in terms of the structure of their balance sheets. But these sorts of sums may be generally regarded as small, if not minimal, by companies such as the giant multi-nationals which make up a significant proportion of the market total. As a result banks have tended to put together syndicates comprising a number of financial institutions in order to raise large sums of money.

During the last year or two there has been a tendency towards rectifying some of the imbalance between lenders and borrowers through the establishment of so-called 'consortia' banks. These are banks whose capital has been subscribed by a number of individual banks, usually from different countries. Hence they are often referred to as 'multi-banks'. The idea is that, by combining the resources of a number of banks in this formal manner, the resources of the consortia bank are raised by a very large amount, giving them a competitive edge against individual banks.

Looking further ahead it would seem safe to assume that the average size of banks participating in this market will grow, either through the consortia route or by mergers. In this manner the relative bargaining strength of the financial institutions will increase over time because of their inability to finance larger proportions of the working capital requirements of the large borrowing companies. Perhaps financial institutions will become more specialised than in the past with larger institutions lending to the multi-national corporations and the smaller and medium size banks lending to other companies, just as has tended to occur in domestic money markets. At the present time, all banks borrowing in the euro-dollar market may be described as 'wholesale' in nature but, over time, some banks will become more wholesale and others less so.

Loans

It is difficult to date changing banking practices with any degree of accuracy as they tend to change over a period of time.

However, taking account of this caveat, it would be fair to say that most loans in the euro-dollar market up to about 1964 were in thirty- to sixty-day category and very few extended beyond six months and even fewer beyond one year. By and large, banks matched their loans with deposits of an equivalent maturity so that the whole structure of the market was really short term. As the demand for longer-term loans grew, banks found themselves, through the pressure of competition, having to extend loan maturities further and further, but this meant that they were exposed to risk as it proved extremely difficult to persuade investors to deposit for increasing periods of time. Thus, if a bank had contracted a loan for (say) one year and had taken deposits with a maturity of only (say) six months but interest rates rose, then that bank could take a heavy loss over the life of that transaction.

As a means of avoiding this danger, the 'revolving credit' was introduced in the market.* Under this type of credit, the interest rate on the loan is refixed on a six-monthly basis depending on the level of interest rates prevailing in the market. Therefore, although the life of the loan might exceed one year, and by a considerable margin, the interest rate risk is strictly limited if not eliminated. The lending bank borrows funds for six months and lends out for a similar period, charging the borrowing customer a margin over the cost of funds. At the end of that six-month period the same transaction is repeated, even though the interest rate level may have changed considerably one way or another. But if interest costs have risen, then the entire burden is transferred to the borrowing company as, in each and every case, the lending bank is quoting a cost to the borrower based on the cost of raising funds itself. Of course, if the bank wished to take a chance and lend for six months but only borrowed for a period of one month, choosing to roll these funds over every month, then it could increase its return if interest rates fell over the six months, but could suffer loss if the reverse occurred. Nevertheless, the point is that the introduction of the revolving credit has enabled banks to commit themselves for longer and longer loans while avoiding the vagaries of interest rate fluctuations. The experience of 1966, when euro-dollar interest rates soared as a result of heavy U.S. bank borrowing in that market, acted as a great incentive to the development of this credit instrument so that, at

* See Appendix A for an outline of a typical euro-dollar credit facility.

the present time, the vast majority of loans have this revolving feature.

The next step came when banks introduced multi-currency clauses into loan agreements. At first loans were strictly denominated in terms of dollars even though the cost of borrowing in other currencies such a euro-sterling, euro-Deutschemarks, etc., was often cheaper. In order to introduce additional flexibility for both the borrower and the lender, banks now usually offer borrowing companies the ability to take the whole or a part of their loan in different currencies. Similarly, from time to time there has been a cost advantage of lending funds in the euro-dollar market by means of an acceptance credit facility whereby the lending bank could discount bills of exchange at the German central bank. (This alternative has been available when the Bundesbank has been encouraging banks to buy dollars.)

Although there is no doubt that the revolving credit facility is by far the most popular lending instrument existing in the euro-dollar market, fixed-term loans of up to five years' duration are negotiated regularly and up to ten years periodically. Usually, when interest rates have fallen sharply (as in 1967, and to 1970 to 1972), the demand to tie up borrowing for long periods at what appears to be low interest rates tends to increase. And, as there are usually some investors willing to take the view that interest rates will fall further, transactions do take place. By and large banks simply act as intermediaries in such a situation, taking on funds for the same maturity period as the fixed-term loan. Even so, they may decide to take a view about the future of interest rates themselves, and so lend for a longer period than they borrow.

Apart from these types of loans, banks grant customers 'stand-by' facilities which give borrowers a great degree of flexibility. The borrower negotiates a line of credit with a bank which is available for use when it suits the borrower. Therefore, if a company wants funds quickly such as in the case of an acquisition, those funds can be made available almost immediately after the negotiations have taken place at a prior date. This is particularly important when conditions in the euro-dollar market are unsettled and it might be difficult for even the very highest quality names to borrow funds. For this privilege of having the right to be able to borrow, companies pay a commitment commission, most generally of about half per cent per annum. This also usually applies for loans on the undrawn portion of the credit so that a commitment commission would be paid if the borrower has only utilised (say) half of the credit made available by the lending bank, but this has come under pressure and is often reduced to $\frac{1}{4}$ per cent per annum. The theory here is that the bank has a contingent liability to lend, so affecting its balance sheet and limiting its ability to undertake other business. Stand-by facilities are also granted by banks to other banks and this became a common feature of the euro-dollar market, but is now less popular. Banks generally feel themselves limited in their ability to make loans for long periods of time, even if the interest rate is adjusted periodically. This reflects fears that at some future date banks would find it impossible to borrow funds because of a seizing-up of the market mechanism while they still have a commitment to lend. Therefore banks arrange stand-by facilities with other banks having spare resources, which cover them for periods up to five years if they need funds in a hurry – in other words the next bank takes the risk of not being able to borrow! This risk is reduced as banks usually have stand-by facilities with branches of banks whose head offices have access to domestic currency of the same denomination as the stand-by facility. For example, a London merchant bank will have a dollar stand-by with a branch of a U.S. bank rather than another London merchant bank.

Given the large size of many borrowers in the euro-dollar market, the only way the banks have been able to service these customers is by putting together syndicates. One bank would typically solicit the lending business and would then farm out a part of the loan to each of a number of other banks. So putting togther a substantial sum of money. This technique has evolved partly because of the relatively small size of many banks, and partly (even for larger banks) to minimise the risk of loss. But there is no doubt that the number of syndications for sums below twenty or twenty-five million dollars has declined considerably. Companies have found consortia banks and the larger individual banks willing and able to lend these sorts of sums from their own resources, which avoids all the delays and paperwork involved in putting together a syndicate. Even when syndicates are put together for smaller sums, then the lead bank has found it difficult if not impossible to extract any management fee for so doing from the borrowing company.

Credit risks and banking margins

One aspect of the increasing degree of competition for lending opportunities in the euro-dollar market has been the lengthening of maturities of loans and the shading of banking margins. As mentioned earlier, loans with lives of eight years and more are now a regular feature of the market, so that such loans have become effective substitutes for long-term bond issues. Usually banks have utilised the revolving credit arrangement, fixing interest rates at six-monthly intervals. However, there have been a number of variants along this general line. On occasion banks have been willing to commit themselves to lend large sums of money and then, at a later stage, sell out participations to other banks in the loan, so, in effect, underwriting the entire credit facility. A few banks in 1969 and 1970 attempted to combine the attractions of a long-term bond issue with the advantage of adjusting the interest rate from time to time. These were the so-called 'floating rate' bond issues which looked as though they were going to have a future, but these hopes have been dashed. Basically the banks made commitments to lend for up to fifteen years but with interest adjusted on a six-monthly basis so that bond-holders were protected from interest rate fluctuations. The idea was, by introducing these particular features, to bring commercial banks into the long-term bond area. Yet, in practice, these floating bonds have proved to be extremely illiquid despite their interest-adjustment feature, with holders experiencing difficulty in selling because of the commitment to provide funds for such lengthy periods of time. Consequently the market for these bonds has died away.

Just as maturities have increased, margins have tended to be reduced for high-grade customers. In 1972 a prime commercial customer was able to borrow funds up to (say) seven or eight years at a $\frac{3}{4}$ per cent margin over the cost of euro-dollar deposits, and sometimes $\frac{1}{2}$ per cent, and the very best names could borrow for (say) five years at a $\frac{3}{8}$ per cent margin. Moreover, it should be noted that this margin declines in real terms as time elapses. The bank receives a fixed dollar flow (e.g. $1,000 per annum) regardless of the basic cost of the loan to the borrower, but this dollar flow is worth less year by year as inflation moves on. Put most concretely, if the costs of running a banking department are rising by 12 per cent a year, then, in today's values, the $1,000 return on the seven year loan is worth only $450 by the seventh year, or a ¾ per cent margin is reduced to an effective ⅓ per cent.

More generally, a number of American bankers have mounted a major attack on what are described as 'unsound' lending practices which are supposedly prevalent in the market. In particular they point to the lengthening maturity terms of loans but note that there are usually no amortisation schedules attached to such facilities. This is in sharp contrast to the practice in the United States market where most medium-term loans have a repayment schedule beginning in the second half of the life of the credit. Amortisation schedules have only been used occasionally in the euro-dollar market because of banking competition for business. If one bank is willing to dispense with such a requirement, then other banks have little, if any, chance of insisting on such a clause in the lending agreement. Even so, this issue of amortisation schedules can be something of a red herring. When a bank decides to lend for a medium or long period of time, then it has to be as certain as possible about the potential credit risk. Whether the loan is for seven years, to be repaid at the end of the period, or for seven years amortisable by half-yearly instalments after (say) four years, the lending bank is still entering into a seven-year commitment and will be writing off a substantial loss if anything goes wrong in the course of the loan at any time up to the end of the seventh year.

The real point is that banks have to accept market competition and decide for themselves whether they want to take the credit risk for the sort of returns then being negotiated in the market. If banks feel that loans have become to long, then the answer is to refrain from lending – rather than trying to reduce the life of the loan by practices which are, in any case, unlikely to be accepted by borrowers. There is no doubt that the decline in banking margins has made more and more banks think seriously about their future participation in undertaking euro-dollar credits. Still, it can be argued that 'unsound' banking practices ensued from the willingness of banks to go along with market terms rather than deciding to gracefully decline lending opportunities. Bankers have shown themselves in need of 'discipline' in their operations as much, if not more so, as commercial corporations.

Similarly, worries are often expressed in the market about the

Changing, Lending and Borrowing Techniques

security of loans, as it is extremely rare for loans to be secured by charges on the assets of the borrowing companies except perhaps in shipping, mining or exploration ventures. At best, the lender will be able to insist on a 'negative pledge' for medium-term loans, which simply means that the borrower agrees not to offer specific security to any other lender or be able to demand repayment if the net worth or working capital of the borrower falls below a particular level. The absence of secured loans partly reflects the high credit standing of most borrowers in the market and partly the impact of competition as no borrower is likely to offer security to one bank if another bank is willing to lend without that security.

Deposits

Unlike on the assets side of the balance sheet there have been relatively few innovations on the deposit side of the banks' balance sheets. Until May 1966, all deposits were non-negotiable in that the investors deposited for a fixed term and had to wait for the deposit to mature before being back in funds. Admittedly, in the early years of the euro-dollar market, there was a range for deposits with maturities stretching out from one day to about one year, but it was not until 1966 that deposits became negotiable. The negotiable Certificate of Deposit* was introduced into London in May of that year, lagging approximately five years behind the introduction of the domestic C.D. in New York. This instrument gives the investors the chance of being able to sell their deposits before the date of maturity, so adding to the degree of liquidity. As a result banks pay slightly lower rates on these instruments than on fixed-term deposits. It is not known what proportion of total deposits in the euro-dollar market are represented by C.D.s, but the Bank of England estimates the total of such deposits in London as $4.5 billion in June 1971 and so, perhaps, it would not be too far wrong to assume that there were $10 billion in the market as a whole, and perhaps a great deal more.

However, for periods beyond one year, virtually all deposits are negotiable as investors want the opportunity of selling their deposits if the need should arise. The market for C.D.s with maturities to five years is a strong one, and for the larger banks there is a

* See Appendix B.

market for seven year C.D.s and occasionally ten years. More recently there have been examples of using the revolving credit technique for deposits with funds being lodged for long periods but with the interest adjusted every six months in line with the London inter-bank rates, thereby giving the bank the security of having long-term funds but also giving the depositor interest rate protection.

Euro-commercial paper

A more recent innovation in the euro-dollar market has been the introduction of euro-commercial paper.* The first issues of such paper were made in June 1970 by the London bank, J. Henry Schroder Wagg and Co. Limited, for three U.S. corporations. There was a gap when no further issues were made for a period of about a year, but in the last quarter of 1971, Schroders, along with Goldman Sachs, introduced additional names to the market. In 1972 more companies joined in the market, including two major oil companies. The euro-commercial paper market is analogous to the commercial paper market which has grown to a substantial size in the United States. The basic *raison d'être* is that, by taking funds from investors and lending directly to corporations, the banking system is by-passed, so reducing the cost of borrowing to the company and increasing the return to the investor. Instead of placing deposits with a bank, and the bank lending to a customer, investors buy the paper issued by the borrowing company. Therefore investors have taken the credit risk of the commercial company rather than the bank. This does tend to increase the degree of credit risk because banks are rarely allowed to default on their obligations as they have central banks standing behind them to rush to their aid. Nevertheless, for the type of company issuing commercial paper, the risk of bankruptcy is relatively small (although the United States' experience with Penn Central is not to be forgotten) and so the investor is able to increase his return relative to that on a bank deposit without accepting a significant deterioration in the quality of the investment. Companies are able to cut out the intermediation of banks except for those banks which actually place commercial paper on their behalf. Because they do not need bank credit, then they can

* See Appendix C.

cut down the cost of raising funds – usually splitting the difference with the investor. A further innovation was introduced in 1972 when General Mills issued Deutschemark-denominated paper.

Unlike in the U.S. domestic market, issuers of euro-commercial paper need not back their paper with 100 per cent stand-by facilities, although most companies choose to do so. Until mid-1971 the United States Office of Foreign Direct Investments did insist that any paper be supported with 100 per cent stand-by with a maturity of one year in order that the borrowing qualify as being 'long term' and therefore count as an off-set to overseas investments by U.S. companies. This requirement was then dropped, enabling the paper market to become a great deal more flexible and maturities of the paper issued in the market have varied from one to six months, with the average being somewhere around three months.

Looking further ahead it is possible that commercial paper will be issued by non-U.S. names in the future and perhaps for longer periods of time as well as in a number of currencies.

5 Credit Creation and the Euro-dollar Market

There are two distinct areas of operation in which the euro-dollar market is involved with the creation of credit. Flows of funds into and out of the market across currency borders influence the respective rates of growth of money and credit of countries so affected – with the exception of the United States itself. Given the large size of the market and the willingness of banks and investors to switch funds into and out of dollars, depending on relative interest rates, the money markets of the major industrial nations have become very closely linked. And, as a result of this linkage, the euro-dollar market has had a significant impact on rates of growth of money supply over a wide geographical area.

By and large there is little dispute either in government or academic circles about the effect of the euro-dollar market on credit creation within national boundaries. On the other hand, there is a good deal of dispute about the amount of credit creation taking place within the actual market. This debate flared up in 1969 and has raged ever since although there had been some discussion of this subject as early as 1964. The point at issue is whether the euro-dollar market acts in a manner analogous to a domestic banking market. In a domestic market with an initial injection of cash, banks can, by making loans and acquiring securities, create deposits by some multiple of the cash inflow, depending on the level of reserve requirements. Thus, assuming a reserve ratio of 10 per cent (so that banks must hold 10 per cent of their deposits in idle cash) an initial injection of $1 million can lead to an overall increase in deposits of $10 million by the process of credit creation (or the redepositing of bank loans). At one end of the scale it has been argued that the 'leakages' of deposits in the system are so great that the amount of redepositing of funds, and hence the degree of credit creation, is very small indeed. But there has been a growing number of academics in favour of the existence of a large credit multiplier operative in the market. The problem is to prove statistically the question at issue one way or the other, but this is next to impossible; partly because of sta-

Credit Creation and the Euro-dollar Market

tistical data problems but also because of a number of conceptual difficulties. Nevertheless, the analysis involved is particularly fascinating as well as of some importance.

1(a) *Domestic credit creation in our individual country*

When interest rates move out of line between money market centres, banks and/or investors are given an opportunity to arbitrage funds by borrowing in one currency and lending in another. If, for example, interest rates are higher in the United Kingdom than in the euro-dollar market, then profit can be made by borrowing dollars at (say) 7 per cent and lending at (say) $7\frac{1}{2}$ per cent in the government securities market in the United Kingdom. Under a fixed exchange rate world this inflow of funds leads to an increase in the U.K. money supply.

Fixed exchange rates used to be officially permitted to vary a maximum of 1 per cent either side of the fixed parity so the central bank had to intervene either to supply foreign currency or buy currency when market pressure brought the actual exchange rates to the limits of the exchange bands. Thus, assuming that a bank had dollars and wanted to use those dollars to buy sterling to invest in the United Kingdom, then its demands for sterling would force up the market price of sterling (in terms of dollars) to the upper limit of the permitted exchange rate band (e.g. to $2.42: £1). As a result, the Bank of England would be obliged to intervene in the market to prevent demands for sterling pushing the exchange rate past the imposed exchange ceiling and would achieve this by buying dollars for sterling.

The net result of this transaction is an increase in the sterling deposit account of the bank selling dollars and an equivalent increase in cash assets of the U.K. banking system at the Bank of England. The Bank of England acquires dollar reserves and so increases its assets but at the expense of reducing its sterling cash balances (or being forced to increase the cash balances of banks as the non-resident holder of sterling opens a deposit with a U.K. bank with a cheque drawn on the Bank of England).

At this stage bank deposits and bank cash would have risen by the amount of the dollar inflow, but the process does not then stop. The U.K. banking system now finds itself in a position of having spare resources in the form of excess liquidity (i.e. cash and deposits are rising together but, seeing that cash reserves against deposits are less than 100 per cent, then the level of reserves has risen by a greater percentage amount than the level of deposits). So, the bank taking the deposit makes loans or acquires securities and, given that the recipient of the loan will deposit funds back in the banking system, then total deposits for all banks will rise further. The next bank will find itself with excess liquidity and so increase its loans, and so deposits in the system as a whole will rise further ... and so on, until deposits have risen by the amount that eliminates the degree of excess liquidity arising from the original injection of cash. That stage is reached when deposits have risen by:

$$\text{New Cash} \times \frac{1}{\text{Reserve Ratio}}$$

In actual practice the impact of an inflow of funds is rather more complicated and partly depends on where the new holder of sterling decides to lodge the funds (as well, of course, on the reaction of the central bank). If funds were switched into government securities and the central bank sold additional debt to the same amount, then the money supply would be left unaffected. This follows because the central bank has been able to absorb the inflow, leaving the domestic banking system totally untouched. Even so, the action of the central bank in selling additional debt would prevent any fall in the level of interest rates and, consequently, the interest advantage of bringing funds into the United Kingdom would remain. Sooner or later funds would find their way into the private sector and give rise to an expansion of the money supply and the general availability of credit. Although the precise mechanics vary from country to country, the basic point is that an inflow (outflow) of dollars leads to a faster (slower) rate of growth of the domestic money supply and availability of credit. The central bank has few courses of action open in these circumstances; it can either allow the inflow to give rise to an expansion in the money supply and bring interest rates in alignment by reducing the level of domestic rates; introduce exchange controls to separate the domestic money market from the influence of the euro-dollar market; or allow the exchange rate to float in the market. But more about these possibilities later.

It should be noted also that the existence of the forward

exchange market simply adds another variable to the equation but does not alter the general drift of the argument. Forward exchange rates are influenced by a variety of forces, such as the covering of future export receipts and import payments as well as by investors protecting themselves against exchange risks. Some observers have seemed to argue that variations in forward exchange rates cancel out any advantages of moving funds to benefit from differing interest rate levels. Apart from the fact that, in many instances investors do not cover the currency acquired by selling dollars forward but prefer to take the exchange risk, one need go no further than point out that arbitrage opportunities on a covered basis in favour or against the United Kingdom or euro-dollars have existed for prolonged periods of time.

1(b) *The Special Case of the United States*

Dollar flows across national boundaries do not affect the money supply or the amount of bank credit available within the United States. Similarly, shifts in sterling holdings of countries outside the United Kingdom leave the latter unaffected, and the same applies to other host currencies. As described on pages 15–17, Chapter 2, euro-dollar transactions are reflected in shifts in the ownership of demand deposits in the U.S. banking system but not in the total supply of deposits. For example, a bank which decides to switch dollars into sterling will surrender its demand deposit in the United States to the account of the Bank of England. It is possible that the Bank of England will actually hold its account with another bank but that simply means that one U.S. bank loses a demand deposit while the other gains by the same amount. Assuming a reversal of this process, with investors selling sterling for dollars to invest in the euro-dollar market, then the Bank of England transfers U.S. demand deposits to the account of the seller of sterling. And, just to complete the picture, a sale of sterling for dollars and a simultaneous sale of dollars for (say) French francs as French interest rates rise above other market rates, will leave the Banque de France with more U.S. demand deposits and the Bank of England with less; but the U.S. banking system will be unaffected.

As in the analysis of the effects of euro-dollar flows on an individual country other than the United States, the picture may be complicated by assuming that the central bank gaining dollars decides to invest in other assets within the United States; but the underlying argument remains as before. If the central bank chose to buy Treasury bills and these were sold direct from the Federal Reserve of New York, then demand deposits (and the money supply) would fall just as in any market operation by the central bank. Yet such a sale by the Federal Reserve would represent a shift in policy designed to slow down the growth of the money supply and this alters the parameters of this discussion – if the Federal Reserve wanted that result then it would take place regardless of the workings of the euro-dollar market.

Mechanically there is only one way in which euro-dollar transactions *by themselves* affect the U.S. banking system and that is through variations in reserve requirements for different types of bank deposits. If a holder of time deposits in the United States decides to shift those dollars into the euro-dollar market because of higher interest rates, then time deposits in the United States will fall while demand deposits rise (the investor can only transfer the demand deposit to pay for the euro-dollars). But reserve requirements set by the Federal Reserve on demand deposits are usually three times the level of reserve requirements on time deposits. (This reflects the higher degree of liquidity on demand deposits.) Thus, as demand deposits rise (although equally offset by a fall in time deposits) required reserves to be held in the Federal Reserve increase sharply, so immobilising part of the banking system's balance sheet and leading to a reduction in the level of deposits. On the other hand, if a recipient of euro-dollar flows chooses to invest in time deposits in the United States, then the process is reversed and required reserves of the banking system fall, which enables the level of deposits to increase.

For a period of time the United States' authorities did allow a loophole in this system by permitting U.S. banks to hold zero reserves against deposits lodged with them and owned by their overseas branches. Euro-dollar deposits acquired by branches and transferred to their respective head offices carried no reserve requirements so that demand deposits, previously requiring reserves when owned by someone other than a branch, became a different animal on purchase by branches. The Federal Reserve stepped in and closed this loophole in October 1969 by imposing reserve requirements on such deposits. Nevertheless, the impact of these differing reserve requirements can be easily exaggerated, especially as the U.S. monetary authorities were hardly likely to allow any significant impact to be felt on the volume of credit and money in the United States by the accident of shifts in euro-dollar flows. The tracing of such efforts is more an academic's delight than the unravelling of an issue of real substance.

1(c) *Global credit creation*

Putting the effects of euro-dollar transactions on industrial countries with those on the United States, it can be readily appreciated that such flows can lead to a global increase or reduction in money and credit, or leave these variables unaffected. Firstly, assume a shift in funds from the United States to the euro-dollar market. The U.S. system is unaffected, but if the banks taking on these deposits decide to switch those dollars into other currencies, then the countries experiencing those inflows find that their money supplies have risen. As a result, a shift in the ownership of U.S. demand deposits has given rise to an expansion in the world's money supply. This, in turn, can have real effects on output and price as well as balance of payments positions. Alternatively, assume that banks decide to reduce their holdings of sterling, francs and the like because of changing interest rate patterns, but, this time, the flow of dollars into the euro-dollar market is picked up by branches of U.S. banks and repatriated to the United States. The money supply of the rest of the world falls but that of the United States does not increase, and so there is a net reduction in global money and credit.

The other limiting case is where flows go out of one country and into another but by-pass the United States completely. For example, assume that interest rates in France rise and those in Germany fall so that banks sell their Deutschemarks for dollars and then sell their dollars for francs. The money supply in France is increased but reduced in Germany, yet left unaffected in the United States and the rest of the world. Thus, on a net basis, global money and credit remain unchanged. Of course, it is the case that reserve requirements on deposits in one country are different from those in another, and so equal shifts in currency flows have differing effects on domestic money supplies; but the basic analysis is not altered, simply the statistical results.

Finally, it must be stressed that the intermediation of the euro-dollar market in moving funds from one country to another has not changed the underlying functioning of the international system. Capital flows occurred before the growth of the market and had exactly the same impact on countries as at the present time. When London acted as the focal centre of the international sterling market, shifts in the direction of sterling flows increased the money supplies of some countries and reduced that of others (but left the United Kingdom as unaffected as the United States today). The major difference that has been made by the euro-dollar market is that the scale and speed of capital movements has increased beyond measure. The market has brought the money centres of the world much more closely together by systemmatising and formalising the international money and credit markets. By so doing it is possible that euro-dollar transactions have assumed a life of their own – or the development of the market and its institutional framework has given rise to the phenomenon of multiple credit creation. Put concretely, the market, through its own transactions, has been able to increase its very size.

2 Multiple credit creation

Can the euro-dollar market manufacture its own dollars? That is the question which has generated much controversy and no little heat.* This problem has no relevance to the question of interbank redepositing of funds. As outlined in Chapter 2, banks operating in the market take deposits and then redeposit those funds with other banks, taking advantage of slight interest rate differentials. But by so transferring deposits, additional dollar liabilities are brought into existence. Realistically, the bank taking on deposit will keep virtually no reserves against that deposit before redepositing, so that reserve requirements impose no limi-

* See, for example, Geoffrey Bell, 'Credit Creation Through Euro-Dollars?', *The Banker* (Aug 1964); Fred H. Klopstock, 'The Euro-Dollar Market: Some Unresolved Issues', *Essays in International Finance, Princeton University*, (Mar 1968) no. 65; Milton Friedman, 'The Euro-Dollar Market: Some First Principles', *Morgan Guaranty Survey* (Oct 1969); Fritz Machlup, 'Euro-Dollar Creation: A Mystery Story', *Banca Nazionale del Lavoro Quarterly Review* (Sep 1970); Helmut Mayer, 'Multiplier Effects and Credit Creation in the Euro-Dollar Market', *Banca Nazionale del Lavoro Quarterly Review* (Sep 1971).

tations on the amount of credit creation. Thus, Euro-bank I takes a $1 million deposit and then deposits that same $1 million with Euro-bank II which then deposits with Euro-bank III, and so on. Each bank has a dollar liability on its books of $1 million, which means that on the basis of an original $1 million demand deposit in the U.S. banking system, $3 million euro-dollar deposits have been brought into existence. Given the absence of reserve requirements which allows banks to on-lend to other banks the full $1 million deposit, theoretically the credit-pyramiding process can continue indefinitely. But this is not the case as, at some stage, a bank takes additional deposits in order to lend to a non-bank outside the circle and this (temporarily) breaks the chain.

The economic significance of interbank transactions and hence deposit creation is limited because, as banks are basically non-spenders (simply intermediaries between final lenders and borrowers, or savers and spenders), there is no influence on the income-generating process. The amount of paper deposits could rise to astronomical levels through interbank transactions, but this would not affect the level of borrowing or spending in countries to any degree whatsoever. Nevertheless, this argument should not be taken too far. The existence of the interbank deposit market does mean that funds can be quickly placed in the hands of those banks with loan demands, which improves the efficiency of reserve allocation.

It is the next stages in the credit-creation process which have caused so much difficulty. Assume that a bank lends to a commercial customer along the line with a demand deposit being transferred to the account of this customer within the United States. The borrower perhaps uses those dollars to acquire French francs to use for working capital purposes in France, and the demand deposit in the United States finishes in the hands of the Banque de France. At that point the euro-dollar deposit-creating process comes to an end as the deposit leaves the system. If the Banque de France chooses to acquire U.S. time deposits or government securities, then no further euro-dollar transactions can take place. But the central bank might decide to redeposit these funds itself in the euro-dollar market, enabling the process to continue. Similarly, the dollars originally sold for French francs might have been acquired by another French company wanting dollars to pay for the importation of German goods. In turn, the

German company might find itself with excess cash resources at that moment and decide to place the dollar deposits in the euro-dollar market.

The current debate is about the degree to which redepositing of deposits takes place after they have initially gone outside the system through the granting of a loan to a non-bank. If a loan helps to generate income by enabling the borrowing company to spend, and that loan creates an additional deposit placed back in the euro-dollar market, then further loans and hence more spending can take place. The euro-dollar market is having a real influence on the level of world economic activity.

Some economists have suggested that the euro-dollar market works in a precisely analogous fashion to that of a domestic banking system. More specifically, they say that it operates like a banking system in a country such as Western Germany, with a large foreign trade sector, and with no exchange control restrictions. They take the view that there is a high probability that dollars advanced by one euro-bank will quickly return to the market in the form of a deposit owned by another party. International companies play a leading role in the economics of most advanced countries and these companies are likely to keep their spare cash within the market to benefit from higher interest rates. Thus, dollar receipts to pay for (say) exports made by these companies, with the dollars emanating from the euro-dollar market, will return almost instantaneously to the market as their deposit accounts are credited. As a result, the euro-bank can then make additional loans which will again have a high probability of being redeposited.

Apart from international companies, many central banks have chosen to keep at least a part of their international reserves in the market and this has greatly increased the degree of redepositing. If, for example, the Bank of England takes in dollars as euro-banks sell dollars for sterling, but immediately reinvests these dollars in the euro-dollar market rather than in New York, another round of lending can take place as described earlier. And, if the chances of redepositing are high, then, theoretically, the amount of dollars that can be created with a given injection of cash into the system is very great indeed, because of the lower reserves held against deposits by euro-banks.

On the other hand, another group of economists have argued

with some vigour that the degree of deposit 'leakage' in the system is so great as to totally invalidate any meaningful comparison with a domestic banking system. They point out that borrowers and lenders of euro-dollars are scattered all over the world, which must reduce the probability of redepositing. Moreover, the argument is used that euro-dollar deposits are only utilised on a small scale for the day-to-day settlement of debts. This is in sharp contrast to a domestic banking system where deposits are used as the basic means of payment for the economy as a whole. Companies receiving dollars in payment for exports will need to convert most if not all of those dollars into local currencies to pay employees' salaries and suppliers' bills. Also, it is pointed out that, given the size of United States exports, there is a good chance that many of the loans granted by euro-banks will finish up in the hands of U.S. companies within the United States. These companies, in turn, are restricted in their ability to redeposit dollars into the market by exchange control regulations, and so the dollars disappear from the euro-system.

Although the economists do not deny that some redepositing takes place, they suggest that banks in the market act more in the manner of financial intermediaries, such as savings banks or building societies, than commercial banks. These institutions take deposits and make loans but do not increase the availability of loans or the supply of deposits by any more than the initial inflow of funds. A savings bank may attract a new deposit of $1 million and may make a loan of $1 million, but that will be that! If the savings bank wants to expand its balance sheet further, then it has to persuade other different holders of bank deposits to switch. It is not denied that financial intermediaries do influence income levels (and the activities of euro-banks fit into this category) but the influence is thought to be limited. To the extent that increased lending of dollars by euro-banks raises income levels, savings will also rise and some proportion of these new savings will find their way back into the euro-dollar market – but very little.

As so often is the case in academic debate, the arguments tend to become polarised and this particular discussion has been no exception. In some ways the problem is that banks operating in the euro-dollar market show characteristics common both to commercial banks and savings banks. Some depositors of funds clearly regard their assets as more of an 'investment' than a 'deposit' nature and, like savings banks, euro-banks do not offer chequing facilities. But this is only part of the story. As the market has grown, more and more companies have come to regard the keeping of liquidity reserves in the market as in the normal course of events rather than as a conscious decision of investment policy. As dollar receipts increase then so do their euro-dollar deposits, with a spread of maturity dates to suit their requirements. Thus, it would be reasonable to argue that as the market has developed the degree of redepositing of funds has also risen.

Nevertheless, it has been the role of central banks that has been crucial in determining the amount of credit creation. Sooner or later a euro-dollar loan is likely to finish up in the hands of a central bank somewhere around the world, and the question is whether that central bank decides to redeposit in the market. Again, as a long-term trend, more and more central banks have been keeping a part of their reserves in the market. Not surprisingly, the involvement of central banks in the market has increased most sharply during those periods when euro-dollar interest rates were much higher than interest rates in New York. When the differentials have been smaller, then the temptation to invest in the market has been correspondingly reduced.

This means that the degree of redepositing, and hence the euro-dollar credit multiplier, has almost certainly varied in size over time, yet showing a long-term upward trend. In 1970 the multiplier must have been very large indeed as so many central banks experiencing dollar inflows were immediately redepositing these sums back into the market. However, when interest rates fell back and central banks recognised the problems they caused by large-scale redepositing, the multiplier was reduced.

Finally, despite any appearance to the contrary, this is not simply an academic debate. The expansion of the euro-dollar market undoubtedly has influenced interest rate levels and money supplies in many countries around the world. By so doing the level of economic activity and prices has probably been affected to an extent, and consequently the lives of people. If a part of that market growth came about as a result of the process of credit creation, then credit creation has had real economic effects. Put the other way round, in the absence of the credit multiplier, the market would have been smaller both in size and overall economic impact.

Moreover, the operation of the credit multiplier has important implications for the future rate of expansion of the market. Assuming (as was certainly the case) that the credit multiplier helped to increase the rate of growth of the market by building on new dollar inflows, the reverse will occur if dollar deposits are to be withdrawn from the market. The phenomenon of leverage works two ways! For example, if the euro-system experiences a net reduction in the level of demand deposits held in the U.S. banking system (its cash base) of $1 million, then the total reduction in deposits could be $3 million or $4 million, depending on the size of the multiplier. On the other hand, that school of economists denying the existence of a credit multiplier would expect a $1 million reduction in the cash base to have no further effects on the size of the market and any market contraction to be slow. The proof of the pudding is in the eating, but the bets should be placed on the existence of a credit multiplier of more than minimal size.

6 U.S. Monetary Policy:
U.S. Banks and the Euro-dollar Market

One of the most profound influences on the euro-dollar market over the last half decade has been that of monetary policy in the United States. Federal Reserve actions in that country have had both a direct influence on interest rates in the market and have induced changes in U.S. bank behaviour which also have affected the market in a major way. Before 1966 U.S. banks took only a nominal interest in the market, with very small amounts of euro-dollars being taken by U.S. branches in Europe for repatriation to head offices in New York. In many ways the market was regarded as alien to the United States, with the senior management of many banks in that country taking a sceptical view of its development and preferring to leave well alone. Part of this reaction stemmed from the lack of understanding by many bankers of how the market worked – they viewed euro-dollars as some form of 'funny money' best left to Europeans.

This did not mean, of course, that those banks with branches in Europe were not dealing in euro-dollars, but the level of business was small and was essentially incidental to the operations of banks within the United States. Only a relatively few of the major U.S. banks actually had offices in Europe and most of those had been established for many years and were an integral part of the London, Frankfurt and Paris international markets.

However, the whole nature of U.S. bank interest in the euro-dollar market began to change in the course of 1966 with the transformation being complete by 1969. This change came about almost entirely because of the monetary policies of the Federal Reserve which squeezed credit conditions in the United States, forcing banks to turn elsewhere for funds. Yet, while the involvement of U.S. banks was born out of necessity in periods of tight money, once entry into the market had been made, euro-dollars came to be regarded as a normal alternative source of funds and basically the market became closely linked with the U.S. domestic money market.

U.S. Monetary Policy 55

In implementing monetary policy the Federal Reserve relied a great deal in 1966 and 1969 on the workings of the Regulation Q ceiling on interest rates as a means of squeezing the banking system. Under Regulation Q, the Federal Reserve is empowered to set the maximum interest rate which banks can pay on time deposits. As mentioned earlier, this ceiling is normally inoperative as market interest rates are below the maximum permitted by the Federal Reserve, but in times of tight money and rising interest rates the ceilings have come into play with a vengeance.

Essentially the Federal Reserve chooses to reduce the rate of growth of the money supply which, in turn, helps to raise the level of interest rates in the money market. However, while interest rates on Treasury bills, commercial paper and the like, rise, yields on time deposits in the banking system cannot move up above the fixed Regulation Q ceiling. This means that when time deposits mature, investors look around for alternative ways to invest their funds, consequently taking their deposits away from the banking system. It should be stressed that, during the decade of the 1960s the amount of interest-sensitive funds lodged within the banking system rose sharply, mainly because of the introduction of the Certificate of Deposit in 1961. This instrument, showing a high degree of liquidity and attractive interest yields, persuaded investors previously holding commercial paper and savings deposits to invest their funds with banks. Thus, the potential loss of funds by the banking system increased the more banks sold C.D.s.

The Federal Reserve instituted a change of direction in monetary policy in 1966 which led to a run-off of C.D.s in commercial banks not being renewed on maturity. These banks then began to look to the euro-dollar market as a means of offsetting their loss of deposits, so effectively discovering the existence of the euro-dollar market. In total, borrowings from their European branches by head offices rose $2½ billion in the course of 1966 with most of the increase taking place in the second half of the year when the credit squeeze was at its height. Thereafter, as monetary conditions eased, these banks repaid borrowings, but not to the full extent of their additional takings in 1966. In effect, the experience of 1966 allayed most of the fears of bankers in using this market so they began to regard the market as simply another source of dollars to be used when interest rates were attractive. Even when the Regulation Q ceilings were not in play, U.S. banks would increase their borrowings of euro-dollars if those interest rates were lower than the alternative of raising funds domestically or, alternatively, reduce borrowings if those rates were more expensive. By so doing U.S. monetary conditions began to have a major impact on monetary conditions in the euro-dollar market.

Faced with rapidly rising prices and a booming economy, the Federal Reserve instituted an extremely tight money policy beginning in December 1968. Over the next period of twelve months the money supply remained virtually constant and interest rates rose to record levels. But relying of Regulation Q ceilings, rates of interest on C.D.s remained unchanged at a maximum of 6.25 per cent. As a result banks began to lose these deposits, and between mid-December 1968 and mid-December 1969 outstanding C.D.s fell from $24.4 billion to $11 billion, a fall of over $13 billion. It is no wonder, in these circumstances, banks began to search desperately for alternative sources of funds, with the obvious place being the euro-dollar market.

The effect of a run-off of C.D.s on the banking system follows precisely the same lines as a shift of time deposits away from the United States to the euro-dollar market. Even though investors switch their funds from C.D.s to (say) commercial paper issued by manufacturing companies with similar maturities, the banking system does not suffer an overall loss of deposits. What happens is that demand deposits in the system will rise as the recipient of funds from the sale of commercial paper deposits them in a bank. Nevertheless, as explained in Chapter 5, the reserve requirements that must be maintained against demand deposits have been three times as great against time deposits (in mid-1971, $17\frac{1}{2}$ per cent and 5 per cent respectively). This means that banks are faced with the need to find additional reserves and can only do this by selling assets, reducing loans or attempting to find other sources of funds.

So, during the year ending 31 December 1969, faced with this situation, borrowings of U.S. banks from their foreign branches rose by $8 billion to $15 billion, not surprisingly putting intense pressure on interest rates in the euro-dollar market. Despite the fact that banks were paying extremely high interest rates for funds, their branches in Europe were instructed to go into the

U.S. Monetary Policy 57

market and borrow funds for transmittal back to the United States, virtually regardless of cost.

The attraction of such borrowing to an individual bank in the United States was perfectly clear – it gained funds so that it could then continue lending to its customers. However, as explained earlier, this did not apply to the system as a whole. To the extent that one bank gained additional deposits through the euro-dollar route, then another bank in the United States would lose the equivalent amount. The only net advantage to the system resulted from the fact that until October 1969 banks were not required to hold reserve requirements against borrowings from their overseas branches, but this was of relatively marginal importance.

Yet, as more and more U.S. banks began to tap the market by opening branches in London or Nassau, the demand for eurodollars took on the aspect of a defensive operation. In order that one bank should not lose demand deposits through the taking of euro-dollars by another, that bank itself had to bid for funds in the market. Nobody was gaining very much but nobody could afford a net loss!

Nevertheless, it could be argued that the existence of the eurodollar market benefited those banks with overseas branches relative to the rest of the banking system. One group of banks could deflect the squeeze to some extent, which meant that the impact on the rest of the system was increased for a given degree of monetary restriction. This argument was advanced on a number of occasions in 1969 but was probably misplaced. By and large it is only the largest banks in the United States that have overseas branches, and it was these banks that were suffering the largest absolute loss of C.D.s during the credit squeeze. If the euro-dollar market had not existed, then the sharply increased reserve requirements resulting from the shift from time to demand deposits would have resulted in large-scale sales of government securities, which could easily have led to disorderly conditions in the government securities market.

Consequently, any dislocation in the money and capital markets on a major scale would have forced the Federal Reserve to have intervened in the market to supply reserves to offset the effects of C.D. losses, and this could have hampered the degree of restraint imposed by the central bank. In other words, there is only a certain speed at which a banking system can adjust to a shift towards tight money conditions and the existence of a cushion of euro-dollars acted as a safety valve for the system. Perhaps this enabled the Federal Reserve to institute a degree of tightness in excess of what could have taken place in the absence of the euro-dollar valve.

Impact of U.S. bank borrowing in Europe

While the impact of U.S. bank borrowings of euro-dollars may have been small within the United States, the same cannot be said for its impact on the euro-dollar market. Virtually the entire excess demand for funds by U.S. banks fell on the euro-dollar in 1966 and 1969. As a result, even though the market had grown to a substantial size by that time, U.S. demands still constituted an enormous proportion of the total level of demand for euro-dollars. By 1969 the market had reached a size of $46 billion with U.S. banks alone accounting for $15 billion of borrowings. Moreover, not only were these demands large in proportion to the size of the market, but the increase in the level of borrowings was very rapid over a short period of time. From just under $7 million at the end of 1968, outstanding borrowings of U.S. banks through their branches exceeded $13 billion by mid-June 1970 and reached a peak of just under $15 billion in August. Thus it was little wonder that a shift in demand of this magnitude had a major impact on the level of interest rates in the market.

In earlier years movements in interest rates of much over 1 per cent were regarded as exceptional, but in 1969 interest rates rose by up to 5 per cent, reaching unprecedented levels by any historical comparisons. Similarly interest rate differentials altered dramatically; before 1969 differentials between domestic money market rates and those on euro-currency deposits usually fluctuated between 1 per cent and 2 per cent in favour of the euro-market, but in 1969, euro-dollar rates rose 3 per cent and more over U.S. domestic money market rates and, in the case of Swiss francs, to 6 per cent. Apart from the increase in the level of euro-dollar rates, interest rates throughout Europe moved up, although by differing amounts. This movement of domestic interest rates came about partly because the level of euro-dollar interest rates induced outflows of funds from countries, thereby automatically tightening monetary conditions, and partly because a number of central banks responded to outflows of funds by raising discount rates to protect the level of their international reserves.

Even though there were other forces at play during 1969 increasing the demand for euro-dollars (notably for speculative purposes), there is little doubt that it was the use of the market by U.S. banks that accounted for the upward bound in the level of interest rates. As these banks were experiencing extremely severe pressures on their liquidity positions, they had to try and find additional funds anywhere they could, so increasing the demand for euro-dollars. Consequently the weight of demands for funds from the enormous U.S. money market bore down on the euro-dollar market. This pressure, in turn, was bound to have a greater impact on euro-dollar interest rates than on domestic U.S. interest rates. Over the year domestic U.S. market interest rates rose only by a little over 2 per cent, or less than half the movement of euro-dollar rates. In other words, the focusing of the demands of banks from a large money market on to a relatively small market magnified the movement of interest rates in the smaller market. However, the difference in size between the domestic market and the euro-dollar market applies far more to the United States than to any European country. As a result, the action of U.S. banks in forcing up euro-dollar interest rates had major effects on European countries where interest rates soared. Not surprisingly many European governments reacted by attacking the policies of the Federal Reserve in particular, and President Johnson's Administration in general, for causing a worldwide escalation of interest rates.

At one level this criticism of the United States simply reflected a European refusal to accept that the United States is bigger than any individual European nation. Any change of policy within the United States inevitably will have a substantial impact on the rest of the world and there is little that the United States can do to alter that fact. Yet, at a more sophisticated level, Europe had an extremely important and totally legitimate criticism to make of U.S. monetary policy in 1969 (which spilt over into 1970 and 1971).

The method by which the Federal Reserve implemented its tight money policy in that period might have been designed to cause the maximum disruption in Europe through the intermediation of the euro-dollar market. Assuming that the Federal Reserve had dispensed with the Regulation Q ceilings on time deposits, the demand for funds by U.S. banks would have been spread over the much larger U.S. domestic money market. These banks would have bid for funds at home in the attempt to offset the Federal Reserve's policy rather than only have recourse to the euro-dollar market. U.S. domestic interest rates would then have risen rather more than actually took place but still by considerably less than the upward movement of euro-dollar rates. In these circumstances the chances are that euro-dollar rates would have moved in line with U.S. domestic interest rates instead of by twice the amount.

The Federal Reserve responded to these attacks by attempting to arrest escalating demands for euro-dollars by imposing reserve requirements on borrowings. With effect from October 1969, a 10 per cent reserve requirement was introduced on all euro-dollar borrowings by U.S. banks in excess of an earlier base. This base amounted to $10 billion for all banks taken together, although the base was calculated for each bank separately. The imposition of this reserve requirement raised the cost of taking these deposits and so helped to temper any further increases in demands for funds.

While the introduction of reserve requirements on euro-dollar borrowings was a useful initiative by the Federal Reserve, it was not until monetary conditions eased in the United States that banks began to reduce their borrowings to any significant degree. But equally the repayment of euro-dollars inevitably caused further disruptions in Europe and (as argued in Chapter 8) was a major contributing factor to the currency crisis of 1971, presaging the breakdown of the Bretton Woods international financial system. Just as the sharp increase in demand for euro-dollars by these banks forced up euro-dollar rates, the opposite movement had to lead to a reduction in interest rates. And while demands by U.S. banks had meant that dollar holdings of central banks were reduced, repayments effectively led to increases in these dollar holdings.

The Federal Reserve shifted policy gears in early 1970 and began to ease monetary conditions in the United States. The Regulation Q ceilings on time deposits were raised in the second half of January and interest rates began to fall. U.S. banks then found themselves once again in the position of being able to pick up funds in the domestic market, as they could pay interest rates on C.D.s comparable with those on other money market instruments. However, it quickly became cheaper for banks to borrow funds within the United States rather than through the euro-dollar market, with the result that external borrowings were cut back. Between mid-January and mid-April 1970 euro-dollar borrowings fell by $2.5 billion to $11.5 billion and three-month deposit rates in the market fell back to 8 per cent from over 11 per cent. However, U.S. banks began to use the market again in the second quarter of 1970 as U.S. interest rates hardened. But in the second half of the year, interest rates fell once more and borrowings were rapidly curtailed.

Given that, by June 1970, the cost of taking euro-dollars was about $1\frac{1}{2}$ per cent in excess of taking C.D.s with similar maturities, there is no wonder that U.S. banks substituted C.D.s for euro-dollars on a large scale. From June 1970 to December 1971, outstanding borrowings fell $5 billion, which helped to pull interest rates down to around 6 per cent or less than half the level prevailing a year earlier. The pace of repayments accelerated in 1971 as the cost differential remained decidedly against euro-dollars, and between December 1970 and May 1971 borrowings fell a further $5.5 billion to $2 billion, the lowest level since early 1966.

The $10 billion reduction in U.S. bank demands for euro-dollars occurred despite efforts by the Federal Reserve to moderate the pace of repayments. This unprecedented shift in the direction of capital flows resulted in big capital inflows for various European countries and this was equally as unwelcome as the outflows these countries had experienced in 1969. On November 30th 1970, the Federal Reserve announced that it wanted 'to strengthen the inducement for American banks to retain their euro-dollar liabilities and thus moderate the pace of repayments of euro-dollar borrowings'. The method used was to increase required reserves from 10 per cent to 20 per cent against euro-dollar borrowings in excess of the reserve-free base set in October 1969, which was automatically reduced as borrowings fell. This meant that if U.S. banks continued to repay borrowings but then, at a future date, had to go back to the market, the cost of taking these euro-dollar deposits would be sharply increased. The Federal Reserve hoped that this future threat would make banks think twice before repaying borrowings. Yet these efforts proved to be totally ineffective as U.S. domestic interest rates continued to fall and the cost of maintaining euro-dollar borrowings became prohibitively expensive.

As can be seen from Table 4, there is a reasonably close correlation between variations in U.S. bank borrowings of euro-dollars for transmittal to head offices and euro-dollar interest rates. U.S. bank borrowing is not the only factor influencing euro-dollar interest rates but it has been a major force. From time to time other influences have been dominant as, for example, the demand for euro-dollar borrowings in May and again in August and September 1971 for use in buying European currencies in anticipation of exchange rate revaluations (and even more in 1973). Nevertheless, taking aside these special demands, the pattern of interest rate fluctuations, the upward push in 1969 and the downward pull in 1970 and early 1971, basically reflected the borrowing and repayment of euro-dollars by U.S. banks.

The entry of U.S. banks into the market has meant that the effects of changes in U.S. monetary policy have been felt more immediately and on a greater scale in Europe than ever before. In fact, as argued above, the particular method chosen to implement U.S. monetary policy in 1969 effectively magnified the impact on the rest of the world through the mechanism of the euro-dollar market. Changes in U.S. monetary policy have always influenced interest rates overseas. Before the emergence of the euro-dollar market, international capital flows took place with funds finding their way to centres offering the highest interest rates. The size of the New York money and capital markets ensured that any changes in U.S. interest rates relative to other money market centres would induce movements of capital, thereby affecting interest rates elsewhere. But now, instead of just non-U.S. holders of dollars switching funds between New York and other markets, U.S. banks have entered the picture.

There is little doubt that the upward shift in U.S. domestic interest rates in 1969 would have induced an inflow of funds into New York from investors searching for higher yields and this would have led to a tightening of monetary conditions in the euro-dollar market. But the demands for euro-dollars by U.S. banks ensured that the drain of funds out of the market and into New York took place on an unprecedented scale. The introduction of this new element of demand added to the magnitude of the resultant movements in capital flows and hence of interest rates

TABLE 4

		Liabilities of U.S. banks to their foreign branches	Euro-dollar 3-month deposit rates
		At or near end of month $m	
1966	March	1,879	5.81
	June	1,951	6.09
	September	3,472	7.06
	December	4,036	6.56
1967	March	3,412	5.38
	June	3,166	5.38
	September	4,059	5.78
	December	4,241	6.31
1968	March	4,920	5.44
	June	6,202	6.38
	September	7,104	6.25
	December	6,039	7.13
1969	March	9,621	8.44
	June	13,269	10.50
	September	14,349	11.31
	December	12,805	10.13
1970	March	11,885	8.50
	June	12,220	9.00
	September	9,780	8.38
	December	7,676	6.44
1971	March	2,858	5.44
	June	1,512	7.12
	September	2,475	7.75
	December	909	5.75
1972	March	1,532	5.44
	June	1,443	5.25
	September	2,023	6.00
	December	1,400	5.88

in the market. Similarly, a fall in the level of interest rates in the United States, such as took place in 1970, would have normally led to an outflow of funds but not on anything like the scale that followed when U.S. banks repaid their borrowings.

Obviously the level of demand for euro-dollars by U.S. banks was artificially increased by the existence of the Regulation Q interest rate ceilings. Even so, without the impact of those ceilings, the effect of changes in U.S. interest rates would still be felt in the market. Having once discovered the euro-dollar market, U.S. banks naturally arbitrage between New York and Europe, taking dollars wherever the cost is the lowest. Therefore deposit rates in the United States introduce an effective floor to euro-dollar deposit rates. If deposit rates in the euro-dollar market were to fall below equivalent deposit rates in the United States, U.S. branches in Europe would pick up additional dollars and on a sufficient scale to push those rates back up in line with U.S. rates This does not mean that euro-dollar deposit rates can never be higher than U.S. rates – other demands will ensure that some premium exists. But U.S. banks, going into and out of the market, depending on U.S. monetary developments, establish a floor and act as a major influence determining the direction of movement in the level of interest rates. The euro-dollar market is more than an appendage to the New York money market, but the linkage is very close and the degree of independence of the euro-dollar market from New York is limited.

Similarly, the equation holds on the supply side of the market as, by and large, no holder of dollars will lodge those funds in the euro-dollar market if a higher return can be obtained by depositing directly in New York. Hence, if interest rates rise in New York, funds will tend to shift between the two markets leading to a rise in euro-dollar rates. The correlation between U.S. money market interest rates and euro-dollar rates for both supply and demand reasons is extremely close (as can be seen in the chart on p. 65).

Capital flows and the United States' balance of payments

The U.S. balance-of-payments position is defined on two bases although neither is satisfactory (or even helpful) in indicating underlying developments. The balance on 'official reserve transaction is measured by changes in monetary reserves and selected liabilities to monetary authorities. Thus, if overseas central banks experience a reduction in their dollar reserves as capital moves from Europe to the United States, the balance of payments improves. On the other hand, if capital flows the other way so that overseas central banks pick up dollars, the balance of payments deteriorates. Alternatively, the U.S. balance-of-payments position is measured on the so-called 'liquidity' basis which is defined by reference to changes in monetary reserves and in liquid liabilities to all foreigners, private and official.

Largely as a result of U.S. bank operations in the euro-dollar market, the balance of payments on official reserve transactions experienced enormous swings in 1969 and 1971. The increased level of borrowings of euro-dollars by U.S. banks in 1969 meant that some central banks overseas were experiencing capital outflows as investors switched into the euro-dollar market and out of European currencies. Therefore, despite the existence of an underlying balance-of-payments deficit, the U.S. official balance showed a surplus of $2.7 billion, entirely as a result of these shifts in dollar holdings. Obversely, the repayments of euro-dollar

Euro-dollar Holdings of U.S. Banks and Euro-dollar Rates

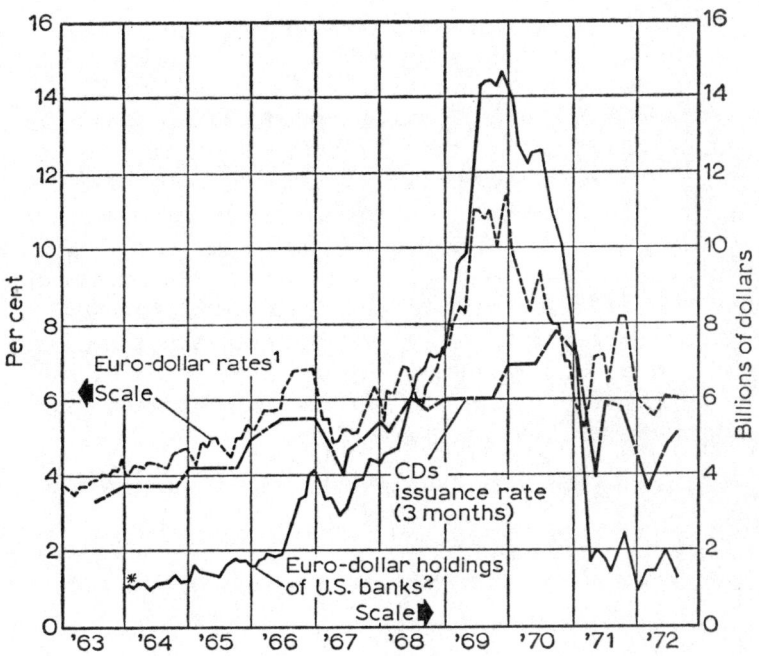

[1] Monthly averages of Friday figures for 90-day euro-dollar rates
[2] Monthly averages of Wednesday figures

borrowings led to dollar accumulations by overseas central banks in 1970 and 1971, so putting the statistical measure of the payments positions heavily into deficit. The deficit amounted to a little under $10 billion for 1970 and $20 billion (at an annual rate) during the first half of 1971, again largely reflecting shifts in capital flows. However, the forces behind these capital flows began to change in 1971 as investors began to sell dollars in anticipation of European exchange revaluations which again had a big effect on the official settlements deficit.

The balance-of-payments position on the liquidity basis is much less affected by capital flows than the other measure. The fact that an overseas central bank gains or loses dollar reserves leaves the liquidity measure unaffected if, as is likely, total short-term dollar liabilities remain unchanged. The ownership of dollar assets may shift from time to time but unless the total level of liabilities is increased or decreased, then the balance of payments does not change.

Given the importance of U.S. bank borrowings over the period 1969 to 1971, there is no wonder that the two measures of what was supposed to be the U.S. balance-of-payments position moved in completely opposite directions. While the official reserve transactions balance improved in 1969 but showed a sharp deterioration in 1970, the liquidity balance worsened in 1969 but improved in 1970. This particular nonsense simply hastened the day of moving away from reliance on any special definition of the U.S. balance-of-payments position. More generally, short-term capital movements associated with the euro-dollar market have made the interpretation of balance-of-payments considerably more difficult and have certainly eliminated the possibility of finding a meaningful and unchanging measure of 'the' balance-of-payments position for any country (even if such ever existed).

7 National Monetary and Exchange Rate Policies

The emergence of a highly efficient market for funds free of controls and of a substantial size has greatly complicated the lives of central bankers around the world. The scale of capital flows has increased beyond measure in recent years as investors and banks have been willing to shift large amounts across national boundaries to benefit from interest rate differentials and possible exchange rate changes. As a result it has been increasingly difficult for any one advanced industrial country to pursue a monetary policy different from that of its neighbours. Basically this has meant that, in general terms, interest rates have tended to move in the same direction on both sides of the Atlantic with the direction being largely determined by the United States.

Additionally the euro-dollar market has had a major influence over the last half decade on the exchange rate policies of European nations. In the past the pressure that could be brought to bear on countries with balance-of-payments surpluses to revalue their exchange rates has been relatively small – in sharp contrast to the case of deficit countries which eventually run out of reserves. However, the euro-dollar market has helped to adjust this imbalance by providing funds to be used for currency speculation. Consequently candidate countries for revaluation have faced the choice of either allowing their exchange rates to rise or be swamped by inflows of funds (such as in Germany in 1969, 1971 and again in 1973). Taking a wider view, it could be argued that the euro-dollar market was a direct contributor to the breakdown of the Bretton Woods system of fixed exchange rates (or, put the other way, that the euro-dollar market helped to usher in a new world of more flexible exchange rates and widespread exchange controls).

1 Monetary Policy

It is not possible for any country to pursue an independent monetary policy in a world of fixed exchange rates and freedom from exchange controls. If a country finds itself with higher interest rates than those prevailing elsewhere, then funds will flow into that country, leading to an expansion of the domestic money supply. The central bank can either allow the inflow of funds to reduce interest rates and remove the incentive to shift funds, or accept a faster growth in the money supply. But the problem is that very often there is a conflict between what is the appropriate monetary policy for domestic economic conditions and what dovetails with international requirements – then something has to give.

The euro-dollar market is central to the system. Domestic interest rates within Europe influence the level of euro-dollar rates but, more importantly, euro-dollar interest rates influence domestic European interest rates. As argued in Chapter 6, monetary policy in the United States exerts a dominant influence on euro-dollar interest rates and this, in turn, affects European monetary conditions. If euro-dollar interest rates are higher than domestic interest rates, then outflows of capital will be induced, helping to push up internal rates or propelling control banks into action to protect their international reserves. Alternatively, if euro-dollar interest rates are lower than domestic interest rates, then funds will flow inwards, pushing up euro-rates while pulling down domestic interest rates. And, as the size of the market has increased, so has its impact on European monetary policy.

It may be pointed out that the euro-dollar market has influenced national monetary policy in one extra dimension as compared with earlier periods. Banks operating in the market have made direct loans in very large amounts to European companies as well as investing in local money market instruments. Therefore, in addition to the normal arbitrage flows between money market assets, direct commercial lending has been injected into the equation and this has increased the scale of capital flows. This factor has been of particular importance in the case of Germany, where non-German investors have found it difficult to find liquid short-term investment outlets for their funds. Without direct loans from euro-banks to domestic companies, Germany would have been in a stronger position in 1969 and 1971 to offset these capital inflows. But the combination of both types of inflows proved to be too much for the monetary authorities.

More generally, direct loans to companies from the euro-dollar market are more difficult for central banks to deal with than straight inflows into money market assets. Companies which borrow are often not very interest-rate sensitive, their only aim being to raise new funds as in periods of really tight money. As a result banks operating in the euro-dollar market are sometimes able to continue finding profitable opportunities of switching funds in local currencies and lending to these companies even if domestic money market interest rates, as on Treasury bills, have fallen back in line with euro-dollar interest rates.

The developments in the European money markets in the second half of 1970 and the early months of 1971 illustrate the force of the euro-dollar market on national monetary conditions. As U.S. banks reduced their outstanding euro-dollar borrowings, euro-dollar interest rates fell back. However, domestic interest rates in most European markets remained unchanged so that euro-dollar rates fell below the levels of domestic European rates. Consequently it became increasingly attractive for companies to borrow in the euro-dollar market rather than through their traditional domestic sources as a means of raising funds. Over the nine-month period to March 1971, short-term euro-dollar borrowings by German companies amounted to an estimated $6 billion. As these companies switched dollars into Germany (or as banks sold dollars to buy D-marks) the reserves of the Bundesbank increased. Also, as the Bundesbank purchased these dollars for D-marks, the domestic money supply rose, helping to frustrate the anti-inflationary policies of the Government.

Apart from this type of inflow, funds were switched into German bank deposits. But, in this instance, the central bank was able to discourage local banks from taking foreign deposits by insisting on the maintenance of high reserve requirements, thereby cutting down the ability of banks to lend out these deposits. Similarly, companies in the United Kingdom borrowed $500 million in the three months ending January 1971 with the pace of new borrowing accelerating almost daily. The Bank of England found that its domestic programme of monetary restraint was being totally breached (the money supply at this time was rising at an annual rate of 10 per cent and so effectively arrested this inflow by insisting that companies only borrow for a minimum period of five years in the euro-dollar market.

Nevertheless, the Bank of England still found it difficult to prevent inflows of funds from leading to a rapid expansion of the money supply as investors switched from the euro-dollar market into government securities and money market assets. It was not until interest rates within the United Kingdom (as in Germany) fell to, and then below, euro-dollar interest rates, that large-scale shifts of funds were moderated. In addition, both central banks increasingly resorted to new measures of exchange controls in attempts to isolate their domestic markets from the influence of falling euro-dollar interest rates.

2 Central Bank Reactions

Central bankers, like other people, want to have their cake and yet eat it! They have wanted to work in a world of fixed exchange rates but still be able to maintain higher or lower domestic interest rates than those prevailing in the euro-dollar market. But short-term funds, like water, find their own level and there is little that even Canute-minded central bankers can do to arrest the forces of the market. As a result they have been forced into introducing artificial barriers designed to stop domestic companies from borrowing euro-dollars and non-resident investors and banks from switching into local currencies. Even so, despite the plethora of exchange controls, central banks have finally been forced to accept the inevitability of abandoning completely fixed exchange rates. Given all the problems of managing a domestic economy, central banks cannot afford to give up the possibility of pursuing an independent line on monetary policy and simply live with interest rate levels or rates of growth of money supply which coincide with those of other countries (and, in particular, the United States). It would be an accident of fortune if domestic and international policy requirements were in harmony for any lengthy period of time, and so central banks have to give themselves at least some area of manoeuvre in the pursuit of monetary policy.

The natural reaction of monetary authorities faced with these problems of capital flows has been to try and isolate the domestic money market through exchange control measures. The French and British authorities have led the way in this respect by insisting that any resident company wanting to borrow in the euro-dollar market must first receive permission from the central bank. As permission can always be withdrawn (or the rate of permissions granted slowed down) the central banks can effectively temper the scale of external borrowing. Also the Bank of England in 1971 required U.K. companies to borrow euro-dollars for a minimum of five years. On the other side, various measures have been adopted designed to stop non-residents acquiring local assets. These have included the prohibition of interest payments or the imposition of such reserve requirements on foreign-owned bank deposits as stops resident banks wanting to take such deposits. Yet the introduction of these types of measures tends usually to lag behind events and often displays more than a little of the 'shutting the stable door after the horse has bolted' mentality. Funds have moved into (or out of) countries before the central bank clamps down with new restrictions.

Before the problem of capital flows became particularly acute since 1969, efforts were made to take away the *raison d'être* for moving funds across national boundaries by co-ordinating interest rate policies among the major industrial nations. The argument put forward was that if each nation gave up some degree of independence in setting domestic interest rate levels, then all nations would benefit. This would lessen the need for erecting exchange control barriers and no one nation would be forced to completely surrender its independence or disappear behind a solid wall of controls. Unfortunately the sucessful co-ordination of interest rate requires that economic conditions be similar both within the separate countries of Europe and between Europe and the United States, and this has not been the case. And, as may be expected, nations put their own domestic priorities first in determining economic policy. Not surprisingly the aim of international interest rate co-ordination simply became a fair weather stategy.

Some economists have argued that even when local economic conditions require differing economic strategies, the conflict issue can be resolved (or reduced) by using fiscal policy for domestic purposes while using monetary policy for maintaining interest rates in alignment with those in other markets. Therefore, if domestic conditions dictate that the economy be slowed down and spending curtailed but that interest rates remain low, in line with those in the euro-dollar market, fiscal policy should be tightened and any resulting upward pressure on interest rates be offset by an easier monetary policy. But fiscal and monetary policies are very closely inter-related and, in practice, it has proved to be next to impossible to achieve this desired end. Tighter fiscal policies usually require an associated tightening of monetary policy and vice versa. Moreover, due to the influence of Professor Milton Friedman and the Chicago School of Economists, opinion has moved in the last few years towards the belief that money policy is a very effective tool of economic management as well as fiscal policy. Consequently governments have become even more reluctant to surrender this arm of policy in the cause of international co-operation.

Given the non-coincidence of interest rate levels among nations, there is only one effective means of securing a degree of independence in the pursuit of monetary policy (apart from establishing an elaborate mechanism of exchange controls) and that is to allow exchange rates to freely fluctuate in the market. In other words, if countries want their interest rates and money supplies to move differently from their neighbours, then the other policy objective of maintaining fixed exchange rates has to be removed.

Allowing exchange rates to fluctuate freely means that central banks keep out of the currency markets so that flows of funds cannot affect local money supplies. If, for example, interest rates are higher in the U.K. than in the euro-dollar market and investors switch into sterling, they have to persuade an existing holder of sterling to part with his funds. Hence, the total supply of sterling is unaffected, one investor's holdings go up while another's fall. Put another way, the impact of any inflow of funds is felt on the level of the exchange rate, which will rise as funds are transferred, rather than on the money supply. This is in sharp contrast to the situation when exchange rates are fixed as the central bank is forced to intervene to buy dollars and sell sterling, so increasing the money supply. The greatest protection of the money supply from external influences occurs when the central bank totally abstains from any market intervention, and the degree of protection is reduced the more the central bank moves towards maintaining a particular exchange parity.

3 Exchange rates

Despite all the efforts of central banks to the contrary, the euro-dollar market has played a considerable role in forcing exchange rate adjustments of countries with balance-of-payments imbalances. Before the market began to assert its influence, the pressure on these countries to devalue was much greater than on countries with balance-of-payments surpluses to revalue. Losses of international reserves tend to concentrate mightily the minds of central bankers and government ministers as each country has a limited amount of reserves. Sooner or later a deficit nation will run out of reserves and so find itself unable to maintain its fixed exchange rate. On the other hand, surplus nations can accumulate reserves for long periods of time before reserves reach levels in excess of any desired amount. Unlike deficit nations which run out of reserves, there is no definite cut-off point for surplus nations at which time action has to be taken.

In addition there are very real pressures within surplus countries not to revalue exchange rates. Revaluation means that the price of exports in foreign markets rises as other countries have to pay more of their currency to buy a given amount of the surplus nation's currency. That change will reduce the overseas demand for exports of the surplus nation, so possibly slowing down the rate of growth of output and raising domestic unemployment levels. Equally, revaluation lowers the price of imported goods in the domestic market of the surplus nation and this benefits consumers but, to the extent that consumers switch to buying more imports and less home-produced goods, local employment can suffer. Such effects can be offset by prompt action by governments designed to stimulate domestic demands, but that requires some luck as well as foresight to achieve a sucessful balance. Perhaps the real point is that producer interests are stronger than consumer interests and governments are reluctant to act against the desires of industrial companies to maintain their export markets.

The euro-dollar market has helped to bring outside pressure on surplus nations to revalue their exchange rates by facilitating large-scale movements of funds into these countries. Because of the market, investors (banks and companies) are able to borrow dollars and sell those dollars for (say) Deutschemarks in very large amounts. They are often willing to pay very high interest rates for loans as the gain from a revaluation more than pays for the interest cost. On the other side of the fence, the central bank of the surplus country finds itself buying more and more foreign currency while selling local currency. Once the pressure begins to mount and people feel that the day of an exchange rate adjustment is getting closer, the pace of currency inflows accelerates very rapidly indeed. Given the existence of the telex machine, enormous sums of money can be moved from one currency to another at a moment's notice. For example, several times in the last few years the Bundesbank bought $1 billion of foreign currency in one day's trading before suspending foreign exchange dealings.

The central bank can try to absorb such inflows by selling government debt but, given the scale of inflows, this is usually very difficult and money market (as well as foreign exchange market) conditions become chaotic. Also the central bank faces a major trading loss on its dollar holdings if a revaluation is to take place as it has been putting out currency at one price only to have to buy it back at a higher price after the revaluation takes place. And, once this wheel begins turning, there is little that central banks can do to change expectations of imminent exchange rate adjustment. Various attempts have been made, such as closing exchange markets for a period of time (as happened all too frequently in 1969, 1970 and 1971), with the monetary authorities hoping that calm would return after period of forced inactivity. Unfortunately for the authorities, the closing of markets more often reinforces expectations of change, and when the markets reopen inflows start again on an ever-bigger scale. Seeing that exchange markets cannot be closed for ever, except at the certain risk of precipitating a collapse in world trade, speculative activities can propel governments to take action on exchange rates. The choice before the authorities is simple: keep the markets closed, or open the markets and buy what currency people want to sell at the old exchange rate, or allow market pressures to raise the exchange rate.

Some countries have been more successful than others in resisting the pressures to revalue despite clear undervaluation of their currencies. The best example has been Japan, which after 15 August 1972 literally stopped any non-resident from buying additional yen through exchange controls. At the other end of the spectrum, Germany has been very reluctant to introduce exchange controls but, consequently, has experienced enormous inflows of funds from time to time.

Basically governments and monetary authorities brought the

problem of capital movements on themselves by being unwilling to adjust exchange rates when their balance-of-payments positions have been obviously out of balance one way or the other. Therefore, because of the delays in exchange rate adjustment, investors have had a one way option to make gains at little cost and no risk. Given the increasing surpluses of a few countries (or deficits of others), there has been no question of which direction the move in the exchange rate would take; the only issues were when and by how much. Faced with the certainty that revaluation (or devaluation) would take place at some stage and, the longer the delay the larger would be the adjustment, it is little wonder that investors have borrowed on weak currencies and bought strong ones. The euro-dollar market provided the currency ammunition while governments created the opportunities for profitable investment.

4 Interest rates, exchange rates and central bank recycling

As may be imagined, flows of funds initially associated with interest rate differentials can generate expectations of exchange rate adjustments as dollars pile up (or are reduced) in the hands of central banks. There is little doubt that the flow of dollars into Germany in 1970 and early 1971, as a result of differences in borrowing costs between the local market and the euro-dollar market, eventually began to reinforce expectations of a revaluation as the Bundesbank announced higher and higher reserve levels. Yet, in addition, the central banks of Europe managed to compound the difficulties associated with the problem of inflows of funds by their own actions. As they took in dollars, the central bankers put them on deposit with the Bank for International Settlements which, in turn, put them straight back into the euro-dollar market. Some central banks even put the funds back in the market directly. And so around and around went these euro-dollars in a bizarre sort of paper-chase. The whole cycle was perpetuated as the gap between domestic interest rates in Germany, the United Kingdom and other European countries remained little altered against the interest rates prevailing in the euro-dollar market. Moreover, as the dollars were deposited and redeposited, the reserves of the central banks (and especially the Bundesbank) were artificially inflated, adding to what were already large inflows. This, in turn, made others in the market believe that decisive action to stem this tide could not be long delayed, and that action would involve revaluations. In other words, a problem of fund inflows resulting from interest rate differentials escalated into a problem for central banks of trying to resist speculative movements of funds. It is difficult to estimate the scale of this double-counting of dollar reserves following the central bank merry-go-round, but some calculations put the amount of 'dollar reserves' created in this way as exceeding $5 billion by the end of 1970, and even more in the early months of 1971.

The experience of countries over the last two or three years has made manifest the point that fixed interest rates and independent monetary policies do not go together. Also, that countries can expect to generate major capital movements if balance-of-payments positions are significantly out of line by creating expectations of exchange rate adjustments. The euro-dollar market has helped to concentrate the minds of governments and central banks on these issues by providing the funds that move across national boundaries. Whatever happens in the future to the international financial system itself, it is clear that, among other things, exchange rates have to be permitted to move more freely either by floating or by more frequent step changes. There are bound to be occasions when interest rates are at varying levels in different countries, depending on local economic conditions. Similarly, balance-of-payments positions themselves will move out of balance from one country to the next. In these circumstances governments will want to avoid inducing movements of funds such as have taken place in the past and this requires, at a very minimum, wider exchange margins along with fixed exchange rates. The possibility that exchange rates can fluctuate up to $2\frac{1}{4}$ per cent above (or below) a fixed exchange parity gives some extra degree of freedom in the pursuit of monetary policy, but as this is not enough governments have moved over to floating exchange rates or two-tiered exchange rate systems, particularly as a means of protecting themselves from speculative pressures. Still, even this is insufficient and governments and central banks have taken the view that these systems must be reinforced by measures to suppress the possibility of movements of capital across national boundaries.

5 Two-tier exchanges and exchange controls

(a) *Two-tier exchange rate systems.* The introduction of two-tiered exchange rate systems became the fashion in Europe subsequent to the August 1971 dollar crisis and, interestingly enough, it was the decision of the Italian Government in January 1973 to join the fashion which triggered off the initial 1973 dollar crisis. By that time France and Belgium were running two-tiered exchange markets and, in a more limited manner (through the investment currency market), so were the United Kingdom and Holland. The idea of the two-tier system is to separate 'commercial' transactions from 'financial' transactions with the government setting the foreign exchange rate in the commercial market and keeping the rate fixed while allowing the exchange rate in the financial market to float up or down according to market forces.

Transactions for which foreign exchange receipts or purchases are made available at the fixed official exchange rates are essentially limited to the current account element of the balance of payments. On the other hand, transactions involving monetary and capital movements have to be financed through the second market. Thus, assuming that a particular currency is undervalued, the idea is that buying pressure will only be manifest in the financial market so that the exchange rate will stand at a premium against the rate prevailing in the commercial market.

Behind the move towards two-tiered systems was the desire of governments and central banks to have their cake and eat it, and this was just another variant on that theme. European governments were anxious to resist upward pressure on their exchange rates because of the fears that revalued currencies would seriously affect their export balances, but they were equally anxious to arrest inflows of unwanted dollars accumulating in their coffers. Recognising that maintaining fixed exchange rates would simply mean that they lost control over their money supplies, but unwilling to go the full distance to floating exchange rates, a number of European governments went to the halfway stage of separating the foreign exchange markets. Basically the hope has been to maintain an official exchange rate which is preferably undervalued (to encourage foreign trade) or at least not overvalued, but, at the same time, to prevent inflows of funds from spilling over into domestic money markets. The latter can only be achieved by a floating rate system with the central bank keeping out of the market. In other words, the thrust of policy is to have a combination of fixed and floating exchange rates.

Also, and apart from the question of at what level the official exchange rate is being maintained, it is felt that foreign trade benefits from having a greater degree of certainty about the future level of the exchange rate than is likely within a general floating system subject to daily exchange rate fluctuations. The argument put forward is that exporters and importers need to be reasonably certain (if only for some limited period of time ahead) of exchange rate levels in order that they price their products sensibly. Put the other way, variations in exchange rates of one or two per cent over a period as short as a week or two, can seriously disrupt pricing policies or cause exporters to suffer losses (or, on the other hand, receive windfall gains).

Obviously there is considerable strength in this case, although the real comparison is not between an official parity which remains stable for long periods of time within a two-tiered system as compared with a floating rate which exhibits wide and unpredictable oscillations. Even when exchange rates between one country and the next are more reasonably aligned than has been the case in recent years, exchange rates have to move to take account of balance-of-payments imbalances so that in either system there can be no guarantee of exchange rate stability. And, when exchange rates are manifestly out of line, there is no difference whatsoever as adjustment must take place regardless of whether that is achieved by floating up or down, or by a change in the official parity. Thus, the issue between the two-tiered school' and the 'floating school' devolves on the advantages of short-term predictability for exchange rate levels against the danger that a two-tiered system has, as it tends to invite governments to delay in adjusting parities so that the eventual movement is more traumatic and difficult than if the market were allowed to push the rate in the desired direction.

Nevertheless, whatever are the pros and cons of two-tiered systems within a reasonably stable currency world, they most certainly cannot work when an exchange rate is distinctly under- or over-valued, or when faced with massive currency flows. Once the exchange rate prevailing for financial transactions is at a substantial premium or discount against the commercial or official exchange rate, foreign exchange operators will find ways of arbitraging between the two markets and the system will cease to function. The exact degree of imbalance between the two markets required to prompt such a development is hard to predict and depends on the strength of administrative controls separating commercial or financial transactions – but a 10 per cent premium or discount is likely to be sufficient. A 10 per cent profit for buying currency in one of the markets and selling it simultaneously in the other is just too tempting. Hence, while France maintained the most elaborate of the two-tiered systems, it was still not sufficiently strong to enable the government to avoid joining in the 1973 revaluation against the dollar once France was faced with very heavy inflows of dollars.

(b) *Exchange controls.* Countries have used a wide variety of exchange controls aimed at suppressing capital flows with the number of controls growing along with the increased magnitude of the problem of currency flows. Exchange controls have been a long-time feature of the European scene with only a few exceptions, the most notable being Germany, but even that country has been forced to erect an elaborate network of controls. Similarly, Switzerland has followed this route and by early 1973 had established a strong control apparatus. Until the late 1960s most of the exchange control devices of European countries were designed to stop *outflows* of foreign exchange, given a background of balance-of-payments problems and low dollar reserves. But this bias had changed dramatically by 1971 and currently the controls are designed to suppress inward movement of funds.

The particular details of exchange controls vary from country to country but basically are divided into three elements; those aimed at:

   (i) discouraging non-residents from opening or increasing local bank deposits;
   (ii) stopping local companies and entities from borrowing abroad and utilising the proceeds at home;
   (iii) limiting non-residents from purchasing local assets, both of a financial and non-financial nature.

All of these controls attempt to stop or temper speculative inflows of funds whereby non-residents try to acquire some asset denominated in the local currency. But, at the same time, the controls discourage inflows of funds of a non-speculative nature but which take place when local interest rates are lower than those prevailing in the international money and capital markets, i.e. arbitrage movements. This gives the local central bank a greater degree of independence in the conduct of monetary policy.

The techniques used to discourage inflows of funds into banks have largely consisted of banning interest payments on non-resident deposits or actually charging non-residents a commission for keeping deposits (negative interest rates). Switzerland, Germany, Holland and Belgium have banned interest payments and Switzerland has charged a commission of 8 per cent per annum on any increases in deposits after June 1972. In addition (or without the interest rate technique as in Japan), central banks have imposed reserve requirements of up to 100 per cent on non-resident deposits taken in by local banks. This means that the central bank neutralises the inflow by taking all the new cash from the recipient banks while removing any incentive for banks to accept deposits. Also, and perhaps most effective of all, the central banks of Japan, Switzerland, Holland and Belgium have placed severe restrictions on the net liability positions of banks in foreign currencies. As a result, while banks accept deposits denominated in dollars, the proceeds can be switched into local currencies except within the prescribed limits – any increase in dollar deposits has to be matched by an increase in dollar loans or other non-domestic assets.

The restrictions of local companies borrowing abroad have taken two forms: those designed to raise the cost of external borrowings above the domestic cost and so remove any incentive to look abroad for funds, or simple administrative controls banning external borrowings. The German Government introduced the 'bardepot' scheme in April 1972 under which domestic companies must deposit interest-free 40 per cent (later raised to 50 per cent) of the proceeds of any external borrowing switched into the country, which means that the effective cost of the borrowing is doubled. However, this type of control proved to be less than fully effective when the external demand for Deutschemarks was strong, as this brought down the cost of D-marks to such a level that even the imposition of reserve requirements could not increase the total cost up to local levels. For example, when the cost of D-mark deposits in the euro-currency market fell to 2 per cent and less for short-term deposits in 1972, the bardepot could not do much to stop German companies from reducing their borrowing costs by going abroad for funds. This, the bardepot had to be backed by administrative controls under which local companies and other bodies had to receive permission from the authorities to borrow abroad – but that permission was just not granted except in very special circumstances. The Japanese, French and Dutch authorities have all used this form of administrative control in preventing this source of currency inflows. Of course, there are always limited exceptions to these and, for example, non-residents have usually been permitted to inject additional permanent capital into operating subsidiaries in most European countries.

Finally, countries have placed stringent restrictions on the ability of non-residents to purchase local assets other than bank deposits (which are covered by the other regulations). Japan has maintained the most complete and effective series of controls. From October 1972 non-residents have been unable to increase their total net investment in Japanese stocks and listed bonds, with purchases of short-term government securities banned even before that date. Similarly, the Swiss authorities froze non-resident investments in Swiss securities at the June 1972 level and insisted that the proceeds of Swiss franc loans made by non-resident companies be immediately converted into other currencies and taken out of the country. Germany also adopted this course of action and stopped non-residents from buying domestic fixed-interest securities in 1972, and restricted purchases of other securities.

The United Kingdom was an exception to this drift towards restricting foreign inflows although on 12 January 1971 the Bank of England introduced Exchange Control 66 which laid down the rule that any local company borrowing funds abroad for use within the United Kingdom borrow for a minimum of five years. For a short period between 31 August and 20 December 1971 it also banned the payment of interest to non-residents on increases in bank deposits. However, by 1973 these rules were being rapidly relaxed as concern mounted about the balance-of-payments situation and in the March 1973 Budget, the government effectively encouraged external borrowing by local authorities and nationalised industries by allowing them insurance cover for the exchange risks involved in such borrowings.

6 *Reserve requirements on euro-dollar deposits*

An alternative method of discouraging capital flows which was much discussed in 1971 was that of introducing regulations directly imposed on banks operating in the euro-dollar market, and a Study Group was set up to examine this subject in June 1971 through the Bank for International Settlements, although nothing has so far emerged. The main set of proposals has centred on whether to impose reserve requirements on euro-dollar deposits as in domestic banking systems. By so doing the cost of taking deposits for banks would increase as a proportion of funds would have to be locked up in relatively low yielding assets such as U.S. Treasury Bills or non-interest bearing assets like cash. As the level of reserve requirements could be varied depending on interest rates in the euro-dollar market, a gap could be maintained between domestic European interest rates and euro-dollar rates. For example, if interest rates in the United Kingdom were 6 per cent and euro-dollar deposit rates 5 per cent but a 20 per cent reserve requirement were imposed, there would be no incentive for banks to take on dollar deposits to switch into sterling. Although they would receive 1 per cent more on their funds by investing in the United Kingdom, they could only switch 80 per cent of any new dollar deposits, with the rest being lodged in non-interest (or low-yielding) reserve assets.

The problem facing central banks wanting to introduce such requirements is to secure a uniform agreement covering all banks operating in the market. Obviously, if reserve requirements were lower for (say) German banks operating in the euro-dollar market than for all other banks, then those German banks could capture all the market by undercutting their competitors. But, even if it were possible to establish uniform controls for European banks, there is no guarantee that non-European nations such as Hong Kong, Singapore, the Bahamas or the Lebanon, would follow suit. As a result the centre of the eurodollar market would move away from Europe, yet the problem of capital flows would still remain as banks would find no difficulty in routing transactions through another centre – all they need is a telex machine and someone to operate it.

8 The Breakdown of the Bretton Woods International Financial System and the Impact of the Euro-dollar Market

The international financial system set up at Bretton Woods in 1944, where the Articles of Agreement of the International Monetary Fund were framed, formally came to an end on 15 August 1971 when President Nixon announced that the convertibility of dollars into gold at a fixed price of $35 per oz. had been suspended. The foreign exchange markets of the western world were immediately closed and when they reopened two weeks later, all the major currencies of the world went over to a more or less floating basis in total violation of the Articles of Agreement of the I.M.F. Some countries allowed their exchange rates to move freely in the market without official intervention (such as West Germany); others intervened on a periodic basis (like the United Kingdom); Japan rigidly enforced the local exchange control requirements but still allowed a small upward adjustment in the exchange rate, and France introduced a two-tiered system in which supply and demand forces were allowed free rein only for certain foreign exchange transactions while others were still conducted at the old official parity.

Thus different countries went their own ways in exchange rate policies and semblance of a structured international financial system disappeared. The basic *modus vivendi* of the I.M.F. world, in which exchange rates would vary a maximum of 1 per cent either side of a fixed parity and that fixed parities would only be adjusted periodically when balance of payments were in so-called 'fundamental disequilibrium' and then to new fixed parities, ceased to operate. The first attempt to put the pieces back together came in December 1971 when, at the Smithsonian Meeting of the major industrial countries, a realignment of currency values against the dollar was agreed along with a small revaluation of the price of gold and a return to fixed parity values. Yet this experiment was short-lived, with the United Kingdom abandoning a fixed rate for sterling in June 1972 and with most countries moving to a more or less floating system in March 1973 along with a further revaluation of gold and currencies against the dollar.

A committee was established under the auspices of the I.M.F. in 1972 to look into the whole question of the reform of the monetary system, but it became quite clear in the course of 1972 and early 1973 that the system had already changed fundamentally in large measure because of the weight of capital movements. And, despite the philosophical objections of a large body of central bankers, a world of floating exchange rates became the order of the day.

Looking to the future, it has become obvious that countries cannot return to the old Bretton Woods system of fixed exchange rates and so exchange will have to move frequently whether or not determined by government decision or by the forces of supply and demand in the market. Moreover, capital movements are likely to continue to be restricted by exchange controls although some countries may permit a greater degree of freedom of monies moving into domestic markets from time to time depending on their balance-of-payments situations. The position of gold in any new system is likely to remain anomalous, with the U.S. Administration continuing to fix the official price of gold and that price could be increased periodically in order to raise the value of official gold stocks and Special Drawing Rights. But the price of gold appears unlikely again to have any meaning in the sense that dollars could be converted into gold at some stated price. Just the symbol will remain.

1 *Background to the 1971 Crisis*

It is too early to ascribe any definitive reasons for the breakdown of the Bretton Woods system and to weight these with any real feeling of confidence. However, three factors stand out: the steadily deteriorating balance-of-payments position of the United States; the reluctance of governments to alter exchange rates up or down until the last moment and the pressure on exchange rates and domestic monetary conditions through capital movements with the euro-dollar market playing the decisive role in this respect. In the absence of a smoothly functioning mechanism for correcting balance-of-payments imbalances, especially between the United States and the rest of the world, the chances were that an impasse would have been reached at some stage, the inevitable outcome being a widespread currency crisis. Nevertheless, it can be argued with conviction that the timing of such a change in the basic functioning of the system would have been postponed had it not been for the weight of short-term funds moving from the United States to Western Europe in 1970, 1971 and 1973. These capital flows brought all the underlying problems of the system into sharp relief.

(a) *United States Balance of Payments.* The balance of payments position of the United States began to show signs of rapid deterioration in the second half of the last decade. Due to the efforts of the Kennedy-Johnson Administrations in implementing tax cuts and the Federal Reserve in allowing the money supply to grow rapidly, the United States began to approach full employment levels towards the end of 1965 (with full employment being defined as 4 per cent of the work force unemployed). By that time extremely heavy defence spending programmes associated with the Vietnam War were being imposed on an economy which was already expanding rapidly. As a result, for the first time since the Korean War, the United States experienced serious inflationary pressures and these pressures have remained ever since. Although foreign trade accounts for little over 5 per cent of total output, the pressure of domestic spending resulted in a sharply worsening balance-of-payments position on current account as imports accelerated much faster than exports. The surplus on the trade account fell from $6.3 billion in 1964 to a deficit (at an annual rate) of $3 billion during the first half of 1971. Much of this deterioration represented the adjustment of the U.S. economy to full employment levels comparable with those of other major industrial nations but a part reflected the effects of inflation and a shift in tastes towards foreign-produced goods.

The deficit on the private long-term capital account ran at between $2 and $2.5 billion a year between 1957 and 1963 but then increased to $3.3 billion in 1963 and to $4.66 billion in 1965 as more and more U.S. companies expanded their direct investments overseas. After the introduction of the programmes to restrict the outflow of U.S. capital and after overseas demands for U.S. securities had picked up, the private capital account improved and actually showed a surplus in 1968. However, this position was reversed in 1969 and 1970 as security prices on Wall Street collapsed and overseas demands for U.S. securities fell off.

Adding to the problems of the United States was the reluctance of other major trading nations to increase the value of their currencies relative to the dollar. Given the re-emergence of Western Europe and Japan as important exporting countries during the 1950s, the relative position of the United States was bound to suffer and its share of world trade in manufactured goods fell from 21.6 per cent in 1960 to 19 per cent by 1970. This declining trend was partly the result of internal developments within the United States but also reflected in no small part the trading advantages other nations secured because of enjoying the benefit of undervalued currencies. Exchange rates established years before had been left little changed although the relative economic position of other countries *vis-à-vis* the United States had shifted. In addition, the increasing over-valuation of the dollar indirectly led to a worsening of the U.S. trade account as domestic manufacturers increasingly set up overseas subsidiaries to manufacture and distribute goods in local markets rather than exporting direct from the United States. Differences in labour costs was one factor in encouraging U.S. companies to go overseas, but the actual over-valuation of the dollar worked to the disadvantage of exporting. This resulted from the adverse pricing effect on U.S. goods when translated from dollars into local currency (i.e. if the local currency had been worth more in terms of dollars, then the price of U.S. goods in local markets would have been lower).

Immediately following President Nixon's August announcement, the Secretary of the U.S. Treasury, Mr John Connally, claimed that the basic improvement needed in the U.S. balance-of-payments position amounted to around $13 billion per year, assuming that the United States were to regain full employment levels. This claim was made despite the fact that only weeks before the most that U.S. Administration officials would admit to was a basic deficit of a few billion dollars. The problems associated with the calculation of the underlying deficit of the United States are vexed because, in addition to statistical difficulties, the question is related to how many dollars the rest of the world is willing to accumulate, and that tends to vary from time to time. But, making allowances for these factors, perhaps it would not be too unfair to suggest that over the year or two prior to 1971, the underlying deficit was running at around $4/$5 billion a year, and was worsening.

The net reserve asset position of the United States deteriorated over a long period of time with the gold stock dwindling rapidly from the late 1950s and onwards. In 1949 gold holdings amounted to almost $25 billion but fell $2 billion in 1950, then remained fairly stable until 1957. Between 1957 and 1970 the gold stock was halved, falling to $11 billion. On the other hand, liquid liabilities to foreigners more than quadrupled over this twenty-year period, reaching $44 billion in 1970 and $52 billion by May 1971. After 1966 and until the end of 1970, liabilities of the United States to banks and other non-official foreigners exceeded liabilities to overseas official institutions, but this position was in the process of being reversed in 1970 and, by mid-1971, liabilities to official institutions were twice the level of liabilities to non-official foreigners. This shift in ownership, as well as the increase in the total level of liabilities, resulted from changing euro-dollar flows. Even though the underlying deficit in the balance of payments was about $6 billion in the year to mid-1971 dollar holdings of overseas official institutions rose by nearly $20 billion, and, for 1971 as a whole, dollar holdings of these institutions rose by $27 billion, with a basic deficit of a little less than $10 million.

The flow of dollars into the hands of overseas official institutions was sharply reduced in 1972, but the basic balance-of-payments position failed to improve, which was the underlying cause of concern about the dollar triggering off the 1973 crisis. Dollar holdings of overseas official institutions rose by around $10 billion in 1972, only one-third of the 1971 increase, but the basic payments deficit was unchanged at $10 billion. Although the deficit was about the same as in the previous year, the components did alter a great deal. Most importantly, the current account showed a deterioration of $5 billion with the deficit on trade account rising from $2.7 billion in 1971 to $6.8 billion in 1972. On the other hand long-term capital inflows were cut back by about $5 billion, so offsetting the deterioration on the current account, while short-term capital flows balanced out for the entire year taken together. Part of the reason for the improvement in the long-term capital account was a big pick-up in foreign purchases of U.S. securities, although these purchases fell off sharply towards the end of the year and in early 1973 as concern about the dollar began to mount.

The fact that the U.S. trade account deficit rose in 1972 caught most observers by surprise, as, following the Smithsonian Agreement with a devaluation of the dollar, some improvement had been anticipated. The deterioration was widely spread geographically but the bilateral trade deficit with Japan grew by over $1 billion to nearly $4 billion. The reasons behind this trade performance in 1972 are not clear except for the usual 'J' curve effects of a devaluation, but the first point is that the lags following exchange rate changes now appear to be generally longer than usually forecast. Moreover, there were at least two additional special factors working against the United States in 1972.

The U.S. economy grew at a considerably faster pace than any of its competitors (other than Japan) in 1972, which was an important factor widening the trade gap as U.S. imports soared along with home demand while U.S. exports encountered relatively depressed markets overseas. In addition, and again related to the state of the economic cycle, U.S. prices increased more rapidly than did the export prices (expressed in local currencies) of most other industrial countries. Japanese prices actually fell, while those of Germany, France and the Netherlands rose by only 1 per cent. Thus, despite the effects of the 1971 dollar devaluation and the fact that the U.S. inflation rate was at least half that of its competitors, the U.S. foreign trade sector still lost out. Yet this was only a temporary phenomenon as the export pricing policies of these countries was related to their need to maintain total sales against the background of slow-growing home economies. The fact is that the effects both of revaluations and domestic inflation rates tend to be passed on to the price of exports sooner or later.

Surprisingly, after the further 10 per cent devaluation of the dollar in February 1973, the fall of the dollar gathered momentum despite the fact that a very large body of opinion believed that the dollar was undervalued, especially against the Dmark and Swiss franc. Yet the upheavals of February and especially the subsequent general move to floating exchange rates fed on themselves and banks, corporate treasurers and the like became extremely nervous and decided to reduce any dollar positions rather than the opposite. The foreign exchange markets became extremely thin which itself added to the slide of the dollar. However, the real test of whether the dollar is undervalued will come in 1974 with a slowing down of the very rapid growth of the U.S. economy which should lead to a cut back in imports.

(b) *Exchange Rate Rigidities.* To suggest that countries have been reluctant to alter their exchange rates is to put the point at its mildest. The struggle of the Labour Government in the United Kingdom between 1964 and 1967 to preserve the value of the pound at $2.80 = £1 took on the dimensions of an heroic battle (in the eyes of the government). The question of national prestige was brought to the fore as it was felt, both by the government and within the Bank of England, that to devalue the pound would be a national as well as economic, financial and moral disgrace. Other countries, in particular the United States, sprang to the defence of the pound, fearing that any breach in the wall of fixed parities would lead to a world-wide chain reaction. (In fact this turned out to be the case, as when one major currency did change its value others immediately became candidates for devaluation or revaluation.) At a different level the British government was rightly concerned about the effect of a devaluation on the rate of growth of the standard of living. A shift of resources was needed away from home consumption into exports in order to improve the balance-of-payments position of the United Kingdom. Success in this regard implied little rise in real wages for a period of time and it was this fact which was of great importance in triggering the later escalation in wage demands and the serious cost-inflation problems of recent years. Wage-earners found it unacceptable that real wages were rising only slowly after the November 1967 devaluation and finally this pressure was translated into increases in money wages.

As argued earlier, surplus countries have shown themselves to be almost as unwilling to alter their exchange rates as deficit countries because of the possible loss of export markets and consequent effects on local employment levels. Given this degree of rigidity on both sides, there is no wonder that balance-of-payments imbalances have been allowed to continue uncorrected for long periods of time. The United States has been unable to act independently in this respect as the dollar acts as the 'numeraire' of the system with currency values being fixed in terms of the dollar and not vice versa. Other countries can change their parities against the dollar but the United States cannot independently fix the value of those other currencies in terms of the dollar.

But, the longer the period of balance-of-payments disequilibrium, the greater has to be the change in exchange rates when the day of reckoning finally arrives. Also the direction of change becomes obvious (the deficit nation has to devalue its currency and the surplus nation revalue) and this generates massive outflows or inflows of funds as investors try to avoid potential losses or make risk-free gains. This brings intolerable strain to bear on the system so that when adjustment is made, countries try to protect their own interests as much as possible with the result that the entire international financial mechanism tends to become fragmented.

For example, the U.K. government in 1967, although having taken the decision to devalue, kept the foreign exchange markets open on Friday 17 November because the formal approval of the Board of Directors of the I.M.F. could not be given until Saturday 18 November. This gesture of abiding by the rules of the game cost the British reserves over $1,100 million on that one day. When the French Government decided to devalue in August 1969 they learned from this lesson and announced the change in parity first and then informed the I.M.F. Under intense pressure from short-term capital inflows, the German government realised in late September 1969 that a fixed parity could not be maintained and so allowed the exchange rate to float upwards and remain floating for a period of several weeks, although in clear violation of the Articles of Agreement of the I.M.F. Canada chose to allow its exchange rate to float freely in the market from May 1970 in an attempt to secure greater independence for its monetary policy, and the German, along with the Dutch authorities, returned to a floating exchange rate once more in May 1971.

Therefore, by May 1971, the payments structure was under intense pressure and the semblance of orderly or quasi-orderly conditions had begun to disappear. The rigid adherence to fixed parities was crumbling and, increasingly, the I.M.F. itself was being by-passed as governments took action which best suited their own book despite the formal rules of the game. Even before the 15 August announcement of dollar inconvertibility into gold, the writing on the wall was clear; the old system was on the way out.

(c) *Role of the Euro-dollar Market.* The repayment of euro-dollar borrowings by U.S. banks in 1970 and 1971 meant that the large inflow of dollars into the euro-dollar market had to be absorbed by someone else and, given the scale of repayments, that someone else had to be European central banks. These repayments led to a reduction of euro-dollar interest rates which then induced European companies to borrow in the market rather than at home. The combination of these borrowings as well as normal arbitrage flows led to sharp increases in the dollar holdings of central banks in general and the Bundesbank in particular. Between May and December 1970, short-term dollar holdings in Germany, as reported by banks, rose from $2.8 billion to $7.5 billion. By February 1971, before speculative pressures began to reinforce these dollar inflows in a massive way, dollar holdings had risen to $8.5 billion, but then shot up to $12.5 billion by May, at which time the German government took the decision to allow the Deutschemark to float upwards, with the Dutch authorities following suit. At the same time Switzerland decided to revalue the Swiss franc by 7 per cent, considerably in excess of what had been anticipated in the market.

These dollar inflows into central banks, associated with interest rate differences and expectations of exchange rate adjustments, were much greater than the volume of dollars entering Western Europe as a result of the underlying U.S. payments deficit. Dollar inflows from the underlying payments deficit were, in fact, perhaps only a quarter of the total dollar flow in Western Europe and Japan over the year to August 1971. In other words, the euro-dollar market greatly compounded the problem of the dollar by providing the funds which moved across national boundaries. The existence of this pool of dollars meant that, as did take place, the ownership of dollars could shift rapidly out of private hands and into the hands of central banks. These inflows directly disrupted the foreign exchange and domestic money markets of countries at the receiving end as well as exposing central banks to exchange risk with their inflated dollar reserves. Following the

March 1968 Washington Agreement on gold, no major central bank could convert dollars into gold at the U.S. Treasury, but they found their dollar holdings accelerating at an extremely rapid pace in 1970 and 1971.

Action needed to be taken and the first move occurred in May 1971 when a few major currencies were allowed to float upwards against the dollar. The second move came in August when President Nixon decided that the only way of securing a major realignment of currency values against the dollar was to cut the knot between the dollar and gold. From then on the dollar itself was floating in the market with its value in terms of other currencies being determined by the responses of other monetary authorities. Given the benefit of hindsight, it was obvious that at some stage a currency realignment had to take place, seeing that the U.S. deficit could not be permitted to continue indefinitely. But the fact that action was taken in 1971 and not 1972 or 1974 was determined in large part by the flows of funds between the euro-dollar and domestic European markets.

2 *European Monetary Integration and Currency Flows*

The international currency crisis in 1971 brought the whole problems associated with any moves towards European monetary integration into sharp relief. The European Economic Community was scheduled to launch the first steps toward establishing a common currency in June 1971, but the May 1971 crisis, when the German and Dutch authorities allowed their currencies to float freely in the market, blasted this proposal out of the water even before the experiment had begun. Another attempt along the same lines began in April 1972 when it was agreed that the maximum exchange rate spread of one E.E.C. currency against any other would be $2\frac{1}{4}$ per cent (or half the permitted exchange margins established under the Smithsonian Agreement). This, in turn, spawned the so-called 'snake in the tunnel', whereby E.E.C. currencies were to move within this narrow band (the 'snake') amongst themselves, but within a wider band of $4\frac{1}{2}$ per cent (the 'tunnel') against the dollar. The idea was that if the strongest E.E.C. currency *vis-à-vis* the dollar was at the top of the tunnel ($2\frac{1}{4}$ per cent above its dollar parity) then no other E.E.C. currency would be below its dollar parity – all had to move together against the dollar. The United Kingdom joined this experiment in May, along with Denmark and later Norway but, just as in 1971, the experiment had a very short history, with the United Kingdom dropping out in June when the pound was allowed to float freely in the market under the pressure of large currency outflows.

The antecedents of European Monetary Union are political not economic, and for many it is the symbol of European unity which supposedly can be achieved without raising too many political obstacles while involving a united front against the U.S. dollar. The big thrust toward E.M.U. followed the creation of the Werner Group in 1971 which laid down the groundwork following a directive issued by the Conference of the E.E.C. heads of government in December 1969. The Werner Group reported in October 1970 and concluded that total economic and monetary integration among the members of the E.E.C. was an objective attainable by 1980, although to be implemented in stages. At the end of the process all principal decisions of economic policy would be taken at the E.E.C. level and national autonomy would disappear. The national central banks and treasuries would become the local monetary and fiscal agents of community-determined policies (just like the Federal Reserve banks scattered around the United States work within the policy objectives determined in Washington). Alongside these moves toward economic integration would be monetary unification including the 'total and irreversible convertibility of currencies, the elimination of margins or fluctuation in rates of exchange, the irrevocable fixing of parity ratios and the total liberation of movements of capital'.

Despite the chequered history so far of E.M.U., yet another attempt in this direction came about in March 1973 when the E.E.C. countries other than the United Kingdom and Italy decided to establish a collective joint float against the dollar, fixing exchange rates amongst themselves but allowing the entire bloc to float against the dollar. The question now is whether or not this new experiment is likely to be any more successful than those in the past – and the chances are not very favourable. The real test will come when one member of the E.E.C. finds itself in balance-of-payments imbalance with one or all of the other members of the Community. In these circumstances the country in payments imbalance will be faced with a choice of trying to correct its imbalance without using the exchange rate or deciding to drop out of the joint float and act unilaterally as a means of correcting its imbalance. Theoretically it is possible that one country in surplus (e.g. France) *vis-à-vis* another (e.g. Germany) will continue to lend funds and so avert the need for the deficit country to correct its payments position, being willing to accumulate Deutschemarks ad infinitum. However, in practice very great pressure would be brought to bear (especially on the deficit nation) to return to equilibrium in the external account. Assuming that exchange rate adjustments are ruled out, the country in deficit could well be forced to accept a considerably higher level of unemployment in order to reduce spending on imports. Alternatively, the country in surplus could be forced to accept a greater degree of inflation so as to reduce its external competitiveness. In either case the outcome is likely to be unacceptable and so countries will choose to use their exchange rates independently.

Nevertheless, there is no question but that the prospects for a successful joint float against the dollar within the E.E.C. are somewhat better given all the capital controls and currency movements both against the dollar and within the E.E.C. Just as Germany has been faced with very large inflows of dollars, the same problem would occur within the E.E.C. if capital were free to move from one part of the E.E.C. to another. For example, the problem of a balance-of-payments imbalance between France and Germany would be compounded by sharp outflows of funds from Germany to France if capital were free to leave the one country and enter another. The recipient country would be no more willing to accept unwanted foreign currency of its neighbour than it has been to accept dollars. But, without freedom of capital movements within the E.E.C., there is little, if any, meaningful monetary integration.

The problem is that the present thrust toward E.M.U. puts the cart before the horse in trying to establish monetary integration within the E.E.C. before establishing fully integrated economic policies. A common currency is the end result of common economic and monetary policies, not the beginning. Agreement has to be reached on harmonising rates of economic growth, balance-of-payments positions and interest levels before the essentials for a common currency unit have been established. Once this has taken place then it is possible to allow capital to float freely from one part of the E.E.C. to another – but not before. But these objectives are extremely difficult to achieve. There is every reason to expect that growth rates and balance-of-payments positions will vary among member countries in the future as in the past and in these circumstances countries will presumably wish to preserve a substantial degree of independence in the conduct of their economic policies, including the ability to change exchange rates. The goal of E.M.U. (permanently fixed exchange rates among member nations without restrictions on capital flows) cannot be achieved unless each country gives up its economic independence and that is a long way off.

9   The Next Phase

The major question mark hanging over the euro-dollar and currency markets is whether the recent rates of expansion of assets and liabilities can be sustained in the future, and the distinct probability is that, at least over the next year or two, growth rates will slow down markedly. The international financial system itself has changed and this has direct bearing on the future functioning of the euro-dollar market. Many of the factors which contributed to the growth of the euro-dollar market were those very features of the system which brought intolerable strains to bear on exchange rate and monetary policies of governments. Clearly, efforts are going to be made to avoid a repetition of these forces and so the environment in which the euro-dollar market will be operating is inevitably going to be less favourable.

Since its early beginnings in the 1950s, the euro-dollar market grew at a remarkable rate with outstanding dollar liabilities rising from $3 billion in 1960 to almost $60 billion (including all currencies) by the end of 1970, and $100 billion by the end of 1972. Even in 1970, when U.S. banks were repaying their euro-dollar borrowings, outstanding liabilities still rose by $18 billion or 30 per cent as European demands then took up the slack created by reduced U.S. demands. The same phenomenon took place in 1971 before President Nixon's August announcement with European demands offsetting U.S. bank repayments, and again in 1972. But what happens if and when U.S. and European demands fall off as can be anticipated?

As usual, interest rates on euro-dollar deposits rose sharply just prior to the August 1971 decision to suspend convertibility of the dollar as investors scrambled to borrow euro-dollars in order to switch these into other currencies in anticipation of upward adjustments in exchange values. The U.S. Administration let its intention of securing an average revaluation of 10 per cent for major currencies against the dollar be widely known. And, just as euro-dollar rates rose sharply, euro-Deutschemark interest rates fell and investors switched into that currency. It took some time for these currency positions to be unwound and it was not really until the latter part of 1971 that euro-dollar rates fell sharply as dollars flowed back into the market and investors took their capital profits. However, the whole process was repeated again in early 1973, with euro-dollar rates soaring as people scrambled to borrow dollars and once again the phenomenon of negative interest rates on euro-Deutschemarks, euro-Swiss franc deposits, etc. was repeated. Following the second devaluation of the dollar anticipations of an early reflow of funds back into the market were widespread, but these expectations were too premature and after the devaluation interest rates remained high on euro-dollar deposits and negative for deposits on other currencies. This reflected a deep-seated feeling of unease about the direction of the entire financial system and a 'wait and see' attitude on the part of investors.

A reduction in growth rates?

Four special factors have been of considerable importance in contributing to the demands for euro-dollars over the last five years. The largest single source of demand for euro-dollars in the short history of the market came in 1969 when the U.S. banks turned to euro-dollar borrowings in an attempt to circumvent the Federal Reserve's tight money policy. That pressure of demand forced up euro-dollar interest rates which, in turn, persuaded many dollar holders to switch their funds out of U.S. assets and reinvest in the market, so contributing to the overall expansion of 50 per cent in the size of the market that year. But those U.S. borrowings were virtually repaid in total by early 1971 and, given all the problems associated with both the borrowing and repayment of these funds, it is most unlikely that the Federal Reserve will ever again permit U.S. banks to use the market on any significant scale.

There is no question but that the introduction of U.S. controls designed to protect the balance of payments added greatly to the demand for euro-currency borrowings on the part of U.S. companies. In 1965 President Johnson introduced voluntary guidelines for U.S. companies, asking them to restrict the flow of funds from the United States for the financing of their investments abroad and, in January 1968, this voluntary programme was superseded by the establishment of the Office of Foreign Direct Investments with the controls made mandatory. From that time forward, except in very limited amounts, U.S. companies had to finance their overseas investments by borrowing externally and they turned to the euro-dollar market. Similarly, since 1965, U.S. domestic banks have been limited in the amount of dollars they could switch overseas because of the Federal Reserve's 'Voluntary Foreign Credit Restraint Programme' under which the Federal Reserve limited any increase in loans to non-residents (which included U.S. companies operating abroad) to 103 per cent of outstanding foreign credits and investments as at 31 December 1964. Also, the U.S. Administration introduced the Interest Equalisation Tax in 1963, which effectively cut off the U.S. capital market for non-U.S. borrowers by raising the cost of borrowing. As a result, non-resident borrowers were forced to raise funds outside of New York and again turned to the obvious source – the euro-currency and euro-bond markets.

The Nixon Administration had begun to ease the OFDI programme in 1972 but it still came as something of a shock to the market when, as part of the announcement devaluing the dollar on 12 February 1973, Secretary Schultz said that 'we shall phase out the Interest Equilisation Tax and the controls of the Office of Foreign Direct Investments. Both controls will be terminated at the latest by December 31st, 1974 . . . I am advised that the Federal Reserve Board will consider comparable steps for their voluntary foreign credit restraint programme. . . . The termination of the restraint on capital flows is appropriate in the light of our broad objective of reducing government controls on private transactions.'. The general view had been that these controls would not be lifted before there had been discernible improvement in the U.S. balance-of-payments position and, of course, it is possible that the timing of the abolition of these controls will be delayed if the U.S. balance-of-payments position fails to show a major improvement by the end of 1974.

Yet bankers operating in the market clearly have to work on the assumption that the controls will be removed and that a large source of demand for euro-currency borrowing will be reduced, if not entirely removed. From that time forth, U.S. companies are likely to turn to their local banks for the provision of funds to finance overseas investments unless interest rates in the euro-currency market are higher than available in the U.S. domestic market. However, on that score the very act of removing controls is likely to ensure that interest rates between the United States money market and the euro-dollar market remain very closely in alignment. Similarly, U.S. banks will be able to service overseas clients (including non-American companies), where exchange controls permit, from domestic sources rather than being forced to operate through their off-shore branches.

Another source of demand for euro-dollars has come from European companies borrowing external funds and converting into local currencies to take advantage of lower interest rates than those prevailing in domestic markets, and this was a major factor in contributing to the rapid growth of the market between 1970 and 1972. These differences in interest rate levels came about both as a result of variations in the levels of economic activity between Europe and the United States and because of changes in the strengths of different currencies. German banks and companies have been in a particularly advantageous position at times when demands by non-residents for Deutschemarks have reduced euro-Deutschemark deposit rates to low (and sometimes negative) levels which, in turn, led to large inflows of funds into the central bank.

Against the deep philosophical leanings of the German authorities, that country had little choice but to resort to exchange control restrictions aimed at preventing arbitrage inflows which grew in intensity in 1970, 1971 and 1972. The particular measure they chose to use was the so-called 'bardepot', or reserve requirement, which sharply increased the cost of external borrowing by requiring companies to deposit a large proportion of these borrowings interest free with the Bundesbank. When even this measure was found to be insufficient, then the bardepot was backed by administrative controls physically stopping companies from borrowing abroad. Similarly, banks were required to maintain high interest-free reserves against foreign deposits, again eliminating any advantage of borrowing abroad and switching into Deutschemarks.

By 1972 every country in Western Europe maintained a barrage of controls, either of market orientation (designed to raise the cost of external borrowing) or of an administrative nature under which permission of the local central bank or Ministry of

Finance to borrow abroad was required, but with this permission being rarely, if ever, forthcoming. The Bank of England chose a different route, insisting that any external borrowings for use in the United Kingdom be for a minimum period of five years and that these borrowings remain unhedged for virtually the entire life of the loan; a device which was extremely effective given that few companies were willing to incur such an exchange risk.

The overall effect of these controls has been to severely restrict arbitrage movements from the euro-currency markets into local money markets. So the West European money markets are now effectively isolated from the international money market and companies have little choice but to rely for their financing on local banks and financial institutions. In other words, the widening of borrowing choices which opened up in the 1960s as the result of the euro-currency market, has now come virtually to an end.

As central banks have learned to their cost, the demand for euro-dollars for speculative purposes has been extremely intense at periodic intervals over the last few years as asset holders have been offered the opportunity of making substantial capital gains. The phenomenon of speculation (or using the more polite term, 'hedging') has grown in volume, especially when it became more and more obvious that European and Japanese exchange rates would have to move up against the dollar, such as in 1971, while central banks were willing to sell their currencies at fixed rates and take in dollars without limit. Adding to this pressure was the growing feeling that central banks could be *forced* to adjust their exchange rates assuming that the weight of currency flows was sufficiently large, and this meant increasingly that banks and companies could not afford to sit back and hold on to dollars in periods when that currency was coming under pressure. Even in cases such as in 1973 when many observers took the view that the dollar was not over-valued against most European currencies, once speculation had begun to escalate, then the experience of previous crises pointed to the fact that another round of revaluations could easily be on the cards, with the result that more and more banks and companies joined in the scramble out of dollars.

Although it cannot be documented with any degree of confidence, it could be argued that the very nature of currency operations changed in the period following the 1967 sterling devaluation. That devaluation, long delayed, had been easy to predict and many operators in the market made substantial profits on what was a one-way option. Then the process was repeated in later years, when even the most myopic of bankers and company treasurers realised that the value of European currencies would have to move up against the dollar. Thus, the foreign exchange departments of many banks became profit centres in themselves, whereas in earlier years these departments had simply been in existence to service clients, with banks generally abstaining from taking currency positions based on the view that that was not their business. Similarly, the treasury departments of large corporations changed in emphasis as many made large profits as a result of currency movements. Of course, corporate treasurers have found themselves in a difficult situation in that they wished to avoid potential losses resulting from exchange rate changes, but there is little doubt that all became much more conscious of the possibilities of exchange rate changes and hence became extremely active in the currency markets.

However, with the introduction of more or less freely floating exchange rates, there is a real possibility that currency movements will be tempered as the risk element is increased. So long as central banks are unwilling to take off funds from the market at pre-fixed prices, currency values can be forced up or down by the market, and the greater the amount of currency variation the greater is the potential degree of risk. Also, with the recent major upward realignments of currencies against the dollar, the next direction of movement of the dollar becomes much more difficult to predict and it is at least possible that over the next few years European currencies will move down against the dollar, and so long as uncertainty remains in this respect then speculation may become less intense.

Following from this point, the future of the U.S. balance-of-payments deficit itself is relevant. Assuming that the U.S. payments deficit is reduced, this means automatically that non-U.S. residents will be accumulating fewer dollars and so have less dollars to deposit in the market. Moreover, to the extent that concerns about the strength of the dollar diminish, more investors will become willing to lodge their funds directly in the United States rather than in the euro-currency markets and so it is possible that even if the overall U.S. balance of payments is in deficit, there will be a net reflow of funds to the United States, thereby reducing the size of the euro-dollar market. Also, with a possible lifting of the controls on the U.S. capital account, interest rates between the United States and the euro-dollar market will become much more aligned and the interest rate advantages that investors have been able to gain by depositing dollars in the external market rather than within the United States will consequently be reduced, so helping this tendency.

Finally, following the experiences of 1970 and 1971 in which central banks, both individually and through the B.I.S., redeposited dollar inflows back into the euro-dollar market, the lesson was learned and the central banks of the major industrial countries refrained from further compounding their problems by such redepositing. Still, other central banks were tempted to maintain deposits in the market and it is estimated that in 1971 approximately $8 billion of deposits in the markets represented holding by official institutions outside the Group of Ten, and it is likely that these holdings grew further in 1972. For example, the foreign exchange reserves of the major oil producers of the Middle East rose by $5¼ billion between the end of 1970 and the end of 1972 and some proportion of this increase is almost certain to have been employed in the market. But increased pressure is being brought to bear on these central banks to reduce their euro-dollar deposits in favour of redepositing directly in New York or in other domestic money markets, all of which could lead to a reduction in the size of the euro-dollar pool.

Moreover, as argued in Chapter 5, the existence of redepositing and the credit multiplier process helped to increase the rate of growth in the market by building up new dollar inflows and, to the extent that such redepositing is restricted in the future, the multiplier will work in the opposite direction. Put another way, the 'leakages' in the euro-dollar system could be greatly increased, so adding to any slowing down of growth in the market.

The absence of these special forces, or a lessening of importance in their contribution to the growth of the euro-dollar market, certainly suggests that the market will expand at a slower pace in the future than in the recent past. Initially there might be an absolute shrinkage in the size of the market as funds flow back to New York and as U.S. companies choose to repay their euro-currency borrowings from increased borrowings from U.S. banks.

At the end of 1972 U.S. companies had an estimated $15 to $16 billion of outstanding foreign debts, of which about 50 per cent consisted of short- and medium-term bank loans, and these loans could be repaid at short notice. The other 50 per cent consisted mainly of long-term euro-bonds and convertible debentures which are more difficult to repay within a short period of time. If this process of euro-dollar repayments begins then there is some likelihood that the market will show a negative period of growth, but once this 'stock adjustment' is completed then the likelihood is that growth will begin once again, albeit at a slower pace.

While it is easy to be pessimistic about the future of the market, this pessimism can be greatly exaggerated. Over the past years the market has benefited from a period of rapid growth in world trade and should continue to do so. Similarly, there will be European and U.S. companies operating outside the existing array of exchange controls and this will add to the demand for loans. Moreover, banks will need the euro-dollar market as a means of adjusting their liquidity positions just as in the past, and the possibility of arbitrage movements both ways across the Atlantic could well be found. For example, with a tightening of monetary conditions in the United States, U.S. banks might well choose to restrict the availability of loans to local companies and these companies are likely to turn to the euro-dollar market as a source of funds, not so much because of interest rate differentials, but because of the availability of credit. Unfortunately, the type of company that is likely to be so restricted by U.S. banks will tend to be those of a more marginal nature, and so banks in the euro-dollar market will be faced with the problem of deciding whether to lend to companies with a lower credit rating than has been the normal pattern for companies utilising the market. Again, given the usual quirks in money markets, arbitrage opportunities will open up from time to time. One problem in this respect is that deals in the euro-dollar market are arranged in such a manner that the dollars are actually delivered with a lag of two days, whereas the sort of arbitrage possibilities that are likely to open up will require the virtually instantaneous movement of funds. Nevertheless, this problem can be overcome and banks may well move over to a basis whereby euro-dollar funds are transferred in New York within a matter of hours after the transaction has been consummated, so that they can deliver funds to U.S. borrowers on the same day.

A shift in the geographical thrust of the market

Perhaps more importantly, the area of most rapid expansion over the next few years seems likely to be outside of the United States and Western Europe and already there is evidence that this business is growing rapidly. In the year to October 1972, London-based banks increased their loans to Latin America, Africa and the Middle and Far East by $6 billion and, based on impressionistic evidence, this rate of growth was even more pronounced in the early months of 1972. For example, the Algerian company, Sonatrach, borrowed $250 million in March 1973 for a period of ten years and, toward the end of the same month, another loan of $300 million for ten years at an interest margin of 1 per cent over the euro-dollar deposit rate was arranged by six U.S. banks on behalf of the Banque Algerienne de Developpement and Banque Exterieure d'Algerie; and long-term loans to countries whose credit ratings sent shivers down the spines of many bankers only a matter of months before, have become much sought after as potential borrowers. Brazil has become the recipient of very large sums of money, with the result that margins of lending for that country have declined sharply with ten-year loans arranged at margins of 1 per cent, and loans have been put together at even finer margins. An illustration of the strength of Brazil as a borrower has been the decision of the Brazilian authorities to insist that any new loan to that country has a minimum maturity of eight years – and bankers have still kept up their pressure to lend.

At the present moment bankers are spreading their lending nets wider and wider, and more and more loans will be made available to those less-developed countries in need of capital but showing political stability. Indonesia and Algeria have just emerged as important borrowers and loans to those countries can be expected to grow apace as bankers look for loans where they can demand margins in excess of 1 per cent for medium-term loans.

The very fact of lending to less-developed countries means that bankers operating in the euro-currency markets are finding themselves directly involved in project financing and consequently in long-term loans up to, and sometimes beyond, ten years. The financing of oil refineries, aluminium smelters, pipelines and the like, is becoming more commonplace, but this represents a very different type of lending business than has been current in the previous life of the market. The difference in lending for such purposes as against the previous practice of providing working capital to U.S. and European giant companies needs hardly be stressed and, not only have the credit risks involved in lending changed, but the political risks of lending to countries are of a totally different order of magnitude. In addition, the maturity imbalance between loans and deposits in the market has, and is, widening with loans increasing in maturity while deposits generally have remained short term. Looking further ahead, this maturity imbalance may well lead to serious problems, assuming that some of the loans turn sour on the lenders.

On the other side of the coin, it looks as though there will be some shift in the geographic sources of deposits in the market, especially as Middle Eastern countries accumulate increased revenues from oil production. As a result those countries in the Middle East may well choose to lend directly to companies requiring capital rather than depositing in the euro-dollar market either in London or in Switzerland. Similarly, now that the Japanese yen has been revalued and the indications are that the Japanese authorities will open up their capital market to non-resident borrowers, the demand for yen-denominated loans on the part of international companies could well increase, making Tokyo a much bigger financial centre. In other words, the sources of direct lending could well become considerably more diffused than in the past when they have been centred largely in London and in Western Europe.

Another implication of these trends is that regional centres for euro-dollar activities will grow in importance as there are very great advantages for banks to have locations close to the borrowing source and this is particularly important for project financing which needs a high degree of supervision to protect the lender. Thus, with the growth in borrowing in the Middle and Far East, Singapore will become increasingly important and already the Asian dollar market has reached a size in excess of $2 billion, but this will be added to enormously as more banks open their doors in Singapore. Again, it is not hard to predict that other regional centres of the market will develop – perhaps Rio de

Janeiro – following in the wake of local capital needs. Put another way, banks operating in the international money and capital markets will need to have operations in a variety of geographical areas of the world if they are to compete effectively for business rather than relying principally on one centre based in Western Europe.

Future for Banks

The two results of recent developments in the euro-currency markets could be the slowing of future growth and a shift in the geographical thrust of the market. As a result of slower growth, the degree of competition extant in the market will increase further as banks find it more difficult to secure lending opportunities. The number of banks operating in the market has expanded very sharply, with over two hundred and fifty banks operating from London alone and each of these banks has to justify its existence. Given that these banks and branches are not to be closed, then their management could take the view that almost any return on euro-dollar activities greater than zero is to advantage. Banking margins have already narrowed and terms of maturity for loans have lengthened, and this took place in a rapidly expanding market. If the environment of expansion is removed (or tempered) the probability must be that terms and margins will become even finer.

This trend opens up the possibility that the smaller banks presently doing business in the euro-dollar market will choose to use their capital resources in other fields. Assuming that banks work on limited deposit-to-capital ratios, then it becomes increasingly difficult for them to earn a return on capital after tax of 10 per cent or more unless they are lending very large sums of money. Office and staff costs do not rise in proportion to the volume of business; it is, for example, just as easy to write a loan agreement for $10 million as for $1 million, but the return to the bank is increased tenfold while the costs of operation are unchanged. The salaries paid to banking officers are the same for larger institutions as for small institutions yet one officer has more ammunition to lend than the other.

Consequently, these smaller banks may choose to drop out of euro-dollar activities or to amalgamate with other institutions to increase their size so that the market becomes concentrated in the hands of large financial institutions. This does not mean that all small banks will disappear as some will become more specialised and find a market in that area but, in terms of share of the market, small- and medium-sized banks will become less important.

The future position of branches of U.S. banks in Europe becomes a matter for some speculation as a high degree of earnings have emanated from their euro-currency activities and, with a decline in lending opportunities in Western Europe, will go a decline in their earnings. Moreover, with a relaxation of the Federal Reserve balance-of-payments guidelines programme, the need for U.S. banks to have branches in existence to tap the euro-dollar market becomes considerably less important. On the other hand, if U.S. banks are going to service their international clients, they must have access within Western Europe to forms of local financing and this becomes the *raison d'être* for having branches in Europe rather than as a means of undertaking euro-currency transactions. Already the major U.S. banks are becoming important in domestic lending within Western Europe (and especially in the United Kingdom) and this trend can be expected to continue with the smaller U.S. banks moving into domestic business, whereas up to now this type of business has been small or virtually non-existent for these banks. The implication is that competition for domestic lending opportunities will lead to a further narrowing of banking margins within the United Kingdom, France, Germany, etc.

Put more generally, it is not going to be possible for banks operating in London to switch funds from one currency to another and thereby lend locally within Western Europe, and companies and banks operating in Western Europe will have to rely on local finance more than in the past. This trend is likely to hasten the formation of closer links among national banks in different countries so that client companies have access to local sources of finance through the same institution. British banks may join with French and German banks through holding companies to service large clients more effectively. This is taking place already through the formation of consortia banks, but this pattern of development is likely to be strengthened in the future.

City of London

The future role of the City of London has been much discussed, especially in relation to the U.K. entry into the E.E.C., and the early assumption that the City would quickly become dominant within the enlarged Community has become distinctly less prevalent. The thrust of this analysis is that the relative importance of the City of London in the international money markets will decline with a shift in the geographic emphasis of the market and the growth of more regional centres engaged in euro-currency activities. The question is whether other business will be substituted to maintain the growth in London-based banking business.

Some British bankers cherish the hope that restrictions on short-term capital movements will be lifted for intra-E.E.C. currency flows, so that a U.K. bank, for example, could borrow French francs and lend them to German companies for use within Germany – in other words, developing what might be described as a 'European euro-market', while restrictions remain in force on the ability to switch dollars in and out of the E.E.C. However, the lessons that have been learned by governments and central banks are likely to postpone the day of free capital movements within the E.E.C. for a long time to come. Just as the Bundesbank has been reluctant to take in dollars, then it will be reluctant to take in sterling, assuming that the United Kingdom were to run into balance-of-payments problems while companies and banks were able to freely move funds out of the United Kingdom and into Germany. Despite the Articles of the Treaty of Rome and the high hopes of governments in moving to European Monetary Union, the need for countries within the E.E.C. to protect the independence of their monetary policy and maintain some semblance of order in the foreign exchange markets means that monies will not be allowed to flow freely across exchange boundaries. In addition, the very introduction of a joint float against the dollar with the maintenance of fixed exchange rates within the E.E.C. reinforces the need to control money movements. Hence, London banks are unlikely to be able to play an 'offshore' banking role within the E.E.C. as they have played in the currency markets more widely, and so British banks will have to open up operations within each of the different countries of Western Europe if they are to maintain their claim of being 'international', or certainly amalgamate or merge with local European banks. Yet British banks do start at a disadvantage against a number of U.S. banks which have already opened up a wide network of branches throughout the E.E.C. Again, the need to expand operations overseas, both within Western Europe and other parts of the world, will pose capital problems for many smaller banks including the London merchant banks.

It would be wrong to over-play this concern about the future of the City of London. London banks will unquestionably open up operations in different parts of the world which will perform the function of business-getting but many of the resultant loans will, in fact, be put together at the head offices in London. Euro-dollar transactions will continue to flow in both directions across the Atlantic and lending opportunities in Eastern Europe are likely to grow apace, just as will the capital demands of oil and gas producers in the North Sea. The opportunities will certainly be offered but, nevertheless, if U.K. banks are to compete effectively against the giant U.S. banks, then they must spread their banking networks more widely around the world and follow the next stage of development of the euro-currency market.

Appendix A

Memorandum Outlining the Operating Procedure of an Advance/Acceptance Credit Facility

1 AMOUNT   To be determined in accordance with the Borrower's needs and in the light of his most recent financial statement.

2 PURPOSE   To provide General Working Capital.

3 TERM   Five Years.

4 AVAILMENTS

(a) By advances in U.S. dollars for periods of 3, 6, or 12 months in minimum amounts and multiples of U.S. $250,000 or, subject to their availability to the Lender, in any other Major European Currency. Such drawings would be subject to three business days prior notice of the intention to draw.

(b) By Bills of Exchange drawn by the Borrower on the Lender to the Borrower's order and blank endorsed, to mature on a fixed maturity date not later than three calendar months from the date of discounting.
When wishing to make or to renew a drawing, the Borrower would notify the Lender accordingly, at least seven days before the proceeds thereof are required, giving all the information relevant to the drawing.

5 RATE

(a) The rate of discount applicable to all drawings by means of Bills of Exchange would be the discount rate ruling on the day on which discounting takes place in the London Market, augmented by the Lender's Margin, expressed as a percentage per annum.

(b) In respect of cash advances as outlined in 4 (a) above, interest would be charged at a rate calculated as being the aggregate of the Lender's Margin and the cost to the Lender of the appropriate currency for a similar period of time and amount in the London Euro-currency market. This rate of interest would be communicated to the Borrower two business days before the proceeds of the related advances are to be made available.

6 DRAWDOWN PROCEDURE

(a) Upon receiving notice from the Borrower of his intention to draw by means of Bills of Exchange, the Lender would take a draft from the supply in his possession and complete it as to amount, dates and commercial clause. He would then accept the draft and discount it and pay the discount proceeds to the Borrower's account with such bank as he will have indicated.

The Borrower's liability to the Lender in respect of such drawings would be recorded on a Draft Account which the Lender would maintain in the appropriate currency in the name of the Borrower.

(b) The Borrower would notify the Lender of his intention to avail himself of cash advances at least three working days before the funds are required, indicating the amount and the tenor of such cash advances and, at the same time, giving disposal instructions. Such notification would have to be promptly confirmed to the Lender by a letter signed in accordance with the terms of the signature cards which the Borrower would have furnished to the Lender.

7 REPAYMENT PROCEDURE

(a) Cover in respect of Bills of Exchange would have to be provided at maturity. Such cover would have to be remitted by the Borrower to such correspondent as the Lender shall, from time to time, name.

8 COMMITMENT COMMISSION A commitment commission will be charged on the daily unutilised portion of this facility at the rate of (to be negotiated) per annum, and will be payable six-monthly in arrears.

Appendix A 113

9 CALCULATION OF DISCOUNT CHARGES AND COMMITMENT COMMISSION AND INTEREST   Discount charges, interest and commitment commission will be calculated on the actual number of days in each period for which such calculation is made on a 360 day year basis.

10 PAYMENT GROSS   All payments of principal, interest and charges and commitment commission are to be made free and clear of and without deduction for any withholding taxes or other deduction required to be made by the Borrower under any law applicable to him.

In the event of any drafts drawn hereunder being or becoming subject to stamp duty under any law, such duty will be payable by the Borrower.

11 CONDITIONS OF PREMATURE TERMINATION OF THE FACILITY

(a)   The acceptance element of this facility will expire and no drafts may be drawn thereunder if any restriction imposed by any authority make it, in the Lender's opinion, impossible for him to continue to hold the facility at the Borrower's disposal on the terms and conditions set out in this memorandum.

(b)   Notwithstanding anything contained in paragraph 4, in the event that any form of central bank reserve or special deposit requirement on or in respect of deposits or loans or acceptance credits expressed in U.S. dollars, or other currency in respect of which availments are outstanding, are imposed by the U.K. authorities, the Borrower will on demand pay to the Lender, by way of additional interest or discount charges, an amount equal to the loss or to the additional cost suffered by the Lender and reasonably attributable by him to such requirement affecting the loans and acceptance credits hereunder, and the Borrower will be entitled, on giving ten business days prior notice to this effect, to terminate this facility by repaying all availments thereunder as they mature.

12 COVENANTS

(a)   This facility is granted on an unsecured basis on the

condition that during its currency, neither the Borrower nor any of its subsidiary companies would grant security in any form whatsoever in favour of any bank in support of any existing or future borrowing providing for repayment in whole or in part before the expiry of this facility.

(b) The Borrower will maintain its relationship between current assets an current liabilities at a ratio of not less than (to be determined). This ratio will be determined in accordance with generally accepted accounting principles consistently applied and, in order to substantiate it, the Borrower will furnish to the Lender a signed statement showing the current portion (due within one year) of the debt with an original term of at least 4 years.

(c) The Borrower will maintain its Consolidated Net Worth (which shall be defined for the purpose hereof as the sum of its paid-up Capital Stock, Legal Reserves and Free Reserves available for distribution, but excluding provisions for Pensions, Contingencies, Depreciation and other provisions and after deducting the amounts, if any, at which Goodwill and the excess cost of subsidiaries acquired over the book value of their Net Assets, and any shares of the Stock of the Borrower or its subsidiaries and other intangible Assets, including any debit balances on Profit and Loss Account which appears or would appear on the Asset side of a Consolidated Balance Sheet of the Borrower and its subsidiaries) in an amount of not less than (amount to be determined).

(d) The Borrower will not permit the aggregate principal amount outstanding of its and its subsidiaries' obligation for Borrowed Monies (such Borrowed Monies are to include money borrowed by it and by its subsidiaries and the amounts which it and its subsidiaries are committed to provide under Bills drawn and/or accepted by it and its subsidiaries against any Acceptance Credits or Bill Discount Facilities or under Guarantees and Indemnities issued by the Borrower or any of its subsidiaries) to exceed (multiple to be determined) the amount of the Borrower's Consolidated Net Worth as defined in sub-paragraph (c) above.

(e) During the currency of this facility there will be no change in the Borrower's equity shareholders.

In the event of any of the above covenants failing to be fulfilled:

(i) the Borrower shall immediately inform the Lender thereof,

(ii) the Lender shall have the right at any time thereafter to terminate this facility and to declare that all borrowings thereunder be due and payable, together with accrued interest, commitment commission, premium (if any) and all other applicable charges, costs and expenses, whether legal or otherwise which have been incurred by the Lender or may be incurred in connection herewith.

During the currency of this facility, the Borrower will provide the Lender with a copy of his Annual Report and Account as soon as this is published, together with a certificate, duly signed, and stating that the above listed Covenants have been observed.

13 EVENTS OF DEFAULT   If any of the following events occur, i.e.:

(a) if the Borrower defaults in any repayment of principal or payment of interest, discount charges, commitment commission or indemnity due hereunder, or

(b) if any representation or warranty made in connection with the execution of this facility or if documentation furnished pursuant hereto shall prove at any time to be incorrect in any material respect, or

(c) if the Borrower shall default in the performance of any other term or agreement contained in the terms of this facility and such default shall continue unremedied for 30 days after written notice thereof shall have been given to the Borrower by the Lender, or

(d) if any obligation of the Borrower for the payment of borrowed money or the deferred purchase price of real property (other than any obligation the liability of which the Borrower is contesting in good faith) is declared by the Borrower's creditor or vendor to be due and payable, and is required to be prepaid prior to the stated maturity thereof or

(e) if the Borrower shall become insolvent or bankrupt or shall cease paying its debts as they mature, or shall make an assignment for the benefit of creditors, or if a trustee or receiver or liquidator shall be appointed for the Borrower or for a substantial part of its property or assets, or if a bankruptcy, reorganisation, arrangement, insolvency, or other similar proceeding shall be instituted by or against the Borrower under the laws of any jurisdiction,

then and in any such event any availments under this facility then outstanding would upon declaration to such effect delivered to the Borrower by the Lender become and be immediately due and payable together with accrued interest and any indemnity due in connection therewith, without presentment or demand, protest or notice of any kind, all of which would be expressly waived by the Borrower.

14 ENGLISH LAW The terms and conditions of this facility would be governed by and construed in accordance with English law, and in accepting this facility the Borrower would agree to submit to the jurisdiction of the English Courts in relation to any proceedings arising therefrom.

Appendix B

NEGOTIABLE CERTIFICATE OF DEPOSIT
A.N.OTHER MERCHANT BANK, LONDON

U.S. $ MATURITY 19   RATE per annum

Interest computed on actual number of days on a 360 day year basis.

No.   LONDON   19

THIS CERTIFIES THAT THERE HAS BEEN DEPOSITED WITH

A.N.Other Merchant Bank, 1 Address Street, London

the sum of   United States Dollars

repayable to BEARER/the order of

on , 19 solely at said offices by their draft or telegraphic transfer on New York, together with interest thereon from the date hereof to maturity only at the rate of per cent. per annum upon presentment and surrender of this Certificate at said offices in London.
Neither the deposit evidenced hereby nor the interest thereon may be withdrawn except on or after the maturity date hereof and upon presentment and surrender of this Certificate to said offices as above set forth.
The obligations of A.N.Other Merchant Bank shall be solely as provided in this Certificate and construed under subject to the laws of England.
This Certificate must be presented for payment through the medium of a banker.

for A.N.Other Merchant Bank

Appendix C

This note has not been registered under the Securities Act of 1933 of the United States of America and the offer or sale thereof in the United States of America, its territories or possessions, or to nationals or residents thereof, may constitute a violation of said Act. This debt obligation is to be treated as the debt obligation of a foreign obligor for purposes of the U.S. Interest Equalisation Tax and its acquisition by a U.S. person shall subject such person to tax liability without regard to any exemption or exclusion in Chapter 41 of the Internal Revenue Code, at the rate of tax applicable upon the acquisition of outstanding stock.

COMPANY X

Serial No. ....

U.S. $.................. LONDON, ..., 197

Maturity Date:..................

For value received, Company X, ..., by this promissory note irrevocably and unconditionally promises to pay to the order of ABC & CO. LIMITED on ...., 197 the sum of ....

.... DOLLARS in lawful money of the United States of America at the office of ABC & CO. LIMITED, London, England or, at the option of the holder, at the principal office of ABC BANKING CORPORATION, New York, U.S.A.

This note and the rights and obligations of the parties hereunder shall be construed in accordance with and be governed by the laws of ....

.... By ....

GUARANTEE (as appropriate)

For value received, Parent of Company X, ..., hereby unconditionally guarantees the payment of this note and all costs, expenses and attorneys' fees incurred in the collection thereof and the enforcement thereof and waives presentment, demand and protest and notice of dishonour and any renewal or extension of such note and consents to any renewal and extension.

By ....

Further Reading

Altman, Oscar L.: 'Foreign Markets for Dollars, Sterling and Other Currencies', *International Monetary Fund Staff Papers*, VIII, no. 3 (Dec 1961) pp. 313–52.
— 'Canadian Markets for U.S. Dollars', *International Monetary Fund Staff Papers*, IX (Nov 1962) pp. 297–316.
— 'Euro-Dollars: Some Further Comments', *International Monetary Fund, Staff Papers*, XII (Mar 1965) pp. 1–16.
— 'Recent Developments in Foreign Markets for Dollars and Other Currencies', *International Monetary Fund Staff Papers*, x (Mar 1963) pp. 48–96.
Aschinger, F. E.: 'The Eurocurrency Market and National Credit Policy', *The Bankers Magazine* (Feb and Mar 1971).
Bank of England: 'U.K. Banks' External Liability and Claims in Foreign Currencies', *Quarterly Bulletin* (June 1964).
— 'The Euro-currency business of banks in London', *Quarterly Bulletin* (Mar 1970).
Bell, Geoffrey L.: 'Credit Creation Through Euro-Dollars?' *The Banker* (Aug 1964).
Bloch, Ernest: 'Eurodollars: An Emerging International Money Market' (C. J. Devine Institute of Finance, Graduate School of Business Administration, New York University, *Bulletin*, no. 39, Apr 1966).
Bloomfield, Arthur I.: 'Official Intervention in the Forward Exchange Market: Some Recent Experiences', *Banca Nazionale del Lavoro Quarterly*, no. 86.
Bolton, Sir George: 'International Money Markets', *Bank of London and South America, Quarterly Review* (Mar 1963).
— 'The International Money Market', *The European Capital Market* (London: Federal Trust for Education and Research 1967) (*Federal Trust Report*).
Brimmer, Andrew F.: *Euro-dollar Flows and the Efficiency of U.S. Monetary Policy: An address before the Conference on Wall Street and the Economy, 1969*, (New York: New School for Social Research 8 Mar 1969).
Brimmer, Andrew F.: 'American International Banking, Trends

and Prospects': an address before the 51st Annual Meeting of the Bankers' Association for Foreign Trade, 2 Apr 1972.

Chase Manhattan Bank: *Euro-dollar Financing* (Apr 1968).

Clendenning, E. W.: *The Euro-Dollar Market* (Oxford, 1970).

— 'Euro-Dollars and Credit Creation', *International Currency Review* (Mar/Apr 1971).

Dach, Joseph: 'Legal Nature of the Euro-Dollar System', *American Journal of Comparative Law*, vol. 13, no. 1 (Winter, 1964).

Einzig, Paul: *The Euro-dollar System: Practice and Theory of International Interest Rates* (London: Macmillan, 1964).

— 'Dollar Deposits in London', *The Banker*, CX (1960) pp. 23–7.

— 'Statistics and Dynamics of the Euro-Dollar Market', *Economic Journal*, LXXI (1961) pp. 592–5.

— 'Recent Changes in The Euro-Dollar System', *Journal of Finance*, XIX (1964) pp. 443–51.

Federal Reserve Bank of Cleveland: *The Euro-dollar Market* (June, 1970).

Federal Reserve Board: 'Euro-dollars: A Changing Market', *Federal Reserve Bulletin* (Oct, 1969).

Friedman, Milton: 'The Eurodollar Market: Some First Principles', *Morgan Guaranty Survey* (Oct 1969) pp. 4–14.

Friedrich, Klaus: 'The Euro-Dollar System and International Liquidity', *Journal of Money, Credit and Banking* (Aug 1970).

— *The Eurodollar System* (Program on Comparative Economic Development Cornell University, Ithaca, New York, 1968).

Fratianni, M., and Savona P.: 'Euro-Dollar Creation: The end of a Mystery Story', *Banca Nazionale del Lavoro Quarterly Review* (June 1971).

Hendershot, P. H.: The Structure of International Interest Rates: The U.S. Treasury Bill Rate and the Euro-Dollar Deposit Rate', *Journal of Finance*, XXII (1967) pp. 455–65.

Hodgman, Donald R.: *Eurodollars and National Monetary Policy* (Irving Trust Company, undated).

Johnson, Norris O.: *Eurodollars in the New International Money Market* (First National City Bank, undated).

Klopstock, Fred H., and Alan R. Holmes: 'The Market for

Dollar Deposits in Europe', *Monthly Review*, (Federal Reserve Bank of New York, Nov 1960).
— 'The Euro-Dollar Market: Some Unresolved Issues', *Essays in International Finance No. 65* (Department of Economics, Princeton University, Princeton, New Jersey, Mar 1968).
— 'Euro-Dollars in the Liquidity and Reserve Management of United States Banks', *Monthly Review*, Federal Reserve Bank of New York (July 1968).
— 'Money Creation in the Euro-Dollar Market – A Note on Professor Friedman's Views', *Monthly Review*, Federal Reserve Bank of New York (January 1970).
— 'The Wiring of the Euro-Dollar Market', *Euro-Money* (Aug 1970).
— 'The Use of Euro-Dollars by U.S. Banks', *The Euro-Dollar*, (Rand McNally, for the University of Wisconsin, Madison, 1970).
Little, Jane Sheddon: 'The Euro-Dollar Market: Its Nature and Impact', *New England Economic Review*, Federal Reserve Bank of Boston (May/June 1960).
Machlup, Fritz: 'Euro-Dollar Creation: A Mystery Story', *Reprints in International Finance* (Princeton University, Princeton, New Jersey, and *Banca Nazionale del Lavoro Quarterly Review* (Sep. 1970).
— 'The Magicians and their Rabbits', *The Morgan Guaranty Survey* (May 1971).
Martenson, G. Carroll: *The Eurodollar Market* (Bankers Publishing Company, Boston, 1964).
Masera, F.: 'International Movements of Bank Funds and Monetary Policy in Italy', *Banca Nazionale del Lavoro Quarterly Review*, LXXIX (Dec 1966) pp. 314–27.
Mayer, Helmut W.: 'Some Theoretical Problems Relating to the Euro-dollar Market', *Essays in International Finance*, no. 79 (Feb 1970).
O'Brien, Sir Leslie: *Address to the Bankers Club of Chicago* (27 Apr 1971).
Prochnow, Herbert (ed.): *The Euro-Dollar* (Rand McNally, 1970).
Scott, Ira: *The Euro-Dollar Market and Its Public Policy Implications*, 91st Congress, 2nd Session, Paper no. 12 (Joint Committee Print 25 Feb 1970).

Swoboda, Alexander K.: 'The Euro-dollar Market: An Interpretation', *Essays in International Finance* (Princeton University, no. 64, Feb 1968).
— 'Multinational Banking, the Eurodollar Market and Economic Policy', *Journal of World Trade Law* (Mar/Apr, 1971).

Index

Africa 102
Altman, Oscar 26–7
amortisation schedule 38
arbitrage *see* interest arbitrage

balance of payments: and the eurocurrency market 4; and exchange rates 77–8; imbalances in 89–91; United States 2, 3, 11–12, 64–6, 85–9
Bank for International Settlements 18, 22–3, 26–7; statistics of the market 20–3
Bank of England 13, 100; and capital investments 69–70; and credit creation 45; market statistics 18–21, 28
banks: characteristics of 51–2; competition between 106–7; mergers between 33; size of funds 33; their place in the market 14; United States 5, 58–64 *see also* central banks, commercial banks *and* euro-banks
'bardepot' scheme 80–1, 99
Belgium 77, 80
borrowing from euro-banks 11, 14
Brazil 104
Bretton Woods system 83–95
British Petroleum 31
Bundesbank 23–6

Canada 90
capital movements and flows 2, 9, 48, 108; and euro-dollars 91; and exchange rates 73–5; and speculation 101; and U.S. balance of payments 64–6; coordination of interest rates and 71–2; in Europe 61; short term 66 *see also* interest arbitrage

central banks 23, 26–7; and capital flows 70–72, 74; and credit creation 44–6, 52 *see also* names of specific banks
Certificate of Deposit 39–40, 55–7, 61, 117
claims, maturity of 29–30
commercial banks 26
competition between banks 106–7
Connally, John 86
consortia banks 33, 107
credit assessment 6
credit creation 42–53; domestic 43–45; global 47–8; multiple 48–53; role of central banks in 52; United States 45–7
credit multiplier 42, 53, 102
credit risks 37–9

depositors 23
deposits 26, 39–40; redepositing of 50, 51, 102
Deutschemark 2; and speculation 12, 31; and the bardepot scheme 80–1; and the domestic money market 23–6
Deutschemark denominated paper 41
devaluation of the dollar 1, 97 *see also* revaluation
developing countries 5–6, 30, 104–6
dollar: devaluation of 1, 97; effect on credit and money supply 44; speculation in 31, 100; transactions 22

euro-banks 9; lending rates 11; working of the system 14–17
euro-bond market 7
euro-commercial paper 40–1, 56
euro-Deutschemark 97, 99

Index

euro-dollar market 2; and Bretton Woods system 91–2; and credit creation 42–53; effect on the U.S. banking system 46; future of 4–6, 102–7; growth of 18–23, 96–7; operating procedure 111–16; origins of 7–12; reserve requirements for 82; sources and uses of 23–9; statistics of 18–21; United States effect on 54–66; working of 12–17
European Economic Community 92–5, 108–9
European Monetary Union 92–5
exchange controls 4, 70–1, 79–82
exchange rates 72–5, 76; fixed 1, 70; floating 1, 72, 77–8, 93–4; policies 67–82; reluctance to alter 89–91; two tier system 77–9

Far East 104
Federal Reserve Board 10, 46, 97, 107; monetary policies 54–66 *passim*
fiscal policy 71
floating rate bond issues 37
France 77, 79, 81, 83, 90
Friedman, Milton 72

Germany: capital flows 68–9, 75, 80; domestic money supply 23–26; exchange rate 90; *see also* Bundesbank *and* Deutschemark
gold 84, 92
governments as borrowers 27

hedging 31, 100
Holland 77, 80, 81

imports 73
Indonesia 104
inflation 85, 89
interbank transactions 49
interest arbitrage 11, 23, 45, 64, 68, 99 *see also* capital movements
Interest Equalisation Tax 11

interest rates 10, 11, 52, 99; domestic 68; effect on borrowing by U.S. banks 56, 58–64; fluctuation 34–5; on deposits 96; United States 62
International Monetary Fund 83–4, 90
investment, borrowing for 5
Italy 4, 77

Japan: banks 31; exchange controls 80, 81, 83; revaluation 74, 105
Johnson, Lyndon 97–8

Latin America 27, 104
lending *see* borrowing
liabilities 29–30
liquidity 6, 14; reserves 52 *see also* reserve requirements
loans 33–6; fixed term 35; maturities 29–30, 32
local authorities as borrowers 27
London 6, 108–9; as a market centre 13–14, 28–9

margins 31, 37–9
maturities: distribution 29–30; lengthening of 37
mergers of banks 33
Middle East 27, 102
monetary policy 67–72
money markets: closing of 74; domestic 3, 23
money supply 52; domestic 3, 26; expansion of 62; Germany 23–26, 69; growth of 42; increase in 43
multi-currency clauses 35
multinational companies 4–5, 27, 33, 50; as speculators 30, 101

New York 64
Nigeria 104
Nixon, Richard 1, 3, 83, 92

Regulation Q 10, 55–6, 60, 63
regulations 9

repayment schedule 38
reserve ratio 42
reserve requirements 9, 46, 57, 60, 82
revaluation 67, 73–9; major countries' dislike of 86, 89–91
revolving credit 34, 37

Schultz, George 5, 98
security of loans 39
Singapore 6, 105
Smithsonian Agreement 1
speculation 3, 11–12, 67, 100; sources of 30–1
stand-by facilities 35–6
Sterling Area 27
syndicates 33, 36
Switzerland: exchange rates 4, 80; revaluation 91

United Kingdom 13, 108–9; devaluation 89, 90; exchange controls 81–2; exchange rate 77, 84; floating pound 92–3 *see also* London *and* Bank of England

United States: and credit creation 45–7; and the euro-dollar market 7–12; balance of payments 3, 11, 12, 64–6, 85–9, 98, 101; banks 5, 28–9, 58–64; deposits from 27; economic growth 88; euro-dollar transactions, effect on 46; inflation in 85; interest rates 62; monetary policy 54–66; net reserve assets 87; world trade 86